OCCASIONAL PAPER 222

P9-BEE-519

Informal Funds Transfer Systems

An Analysis of the Informal Hawala System

A JOINT IMF–WORLD BANK PAPER

Mohammed El Qorchi, Samuel Munzele Maimbo,
and John F. Wilson

INTERNATIONAL MONETARY FUND

Washington DC

2003

Production: IMF Multimedia Services Division
Typesetting: Julio R. Prego
Figures: Martina Vortmeyer

Cataloging-in-Publication Data

El Qorchi, Mohammed.

Informal funds transfer systems: an analysis of the Hawala system /
Mohammed El Qorchi, Samuel Munzele Maimbo, and John F. Wilson —
Washington, D.C.: International Monetary Fund, 2003.

p. cm. — (Occasional paper, ISSN 0251-6365; 222)
A Joint IMF-World Bank paper.
Includes bibliographical references.
ISBN 1-58906-226-4

1. Hawala system. I. Maimbo, Samuel Munzele. II. Wilson, John F.
III. International Monetary Fund. IV. World Bank. V. Occasional paper
(International Monetary Fund); no. 222
HG177.7.E46 2003

Price: US$25.00
(US$22.00 to full-time faculty members and
students at universities and colleges)

Please send orders to:
International Monetary Fund, Publication Services
700 19th Street, N.W., Washington, D.C. 20431, U.S.A.
Tel.: (202) 623-7430   Telefax: (202) 623-7201
E-mail: publications@imf.org
Internet: http://www.imf.org

recycled paper

Contents

The following symbols have been used throughout this paper:

. . . to indicate that data are not available;

— to indicate that the figure is zero or less than half the final digit shown, or that the item does not exist;

– between years or months (e.g., 2000–01 or January–June) to indicate the years or months covered, including the beginning and ending years or months;

/ between years (e.g., 2000/01) to indicate a fiscal (financial) year.

"Billion" means a thousand million.

Minor discrepancies between constituent figures and totals are due to rounding.

The term "country," as used in this paper, does not in all cases refer to a territorial entity that is a state as understood by international law and practice; the term also covers some territorial entities that are not states, but for which statistical data are maintained and provided internationally on a separate and independent basis.

Foreword

This joint IMF–World Bank paper is a timely contribution to the ongoing debate about the operations, benefits, and risks of the informal *hawala* system. In a debate heightened by the events of September 11, 2001, the authors provide a comprehensive review of the system's historical development, the operational characteristics that popularize its use, and the national and international economic and regulatory challenges it poses.

While drawing attention to the legitimate uses of the informal *hawala* system, such as the transfer of migrant labor remittances and humanitarian, emergency, and relief aid to regions where financial systems are either absent or weak, the authors acknowledge the system's vulnerability to criminal activities. They argue that the benefits of speed, low cost, convenience, and potential anonymity associated with the informal *hawala* system can also attract individuals and groups keen to circumvent existing regulations. The authors rightly conclude that addressing the concerns raised by the informal funds transfer systems will require simultaneous improvements in the formal financial sector. In addition to exchange controls, high transaction costs and long delays in effecting money remittances through the formal sector provide major incentives for the existence of the informal funds transfer systems. Thus, an important conclusion of the paper is the need to tackle deficiencies and enhance competitiveness in the formal funds transfer systems.

The authors highlight the complexity of the regulatory issues posed by the informal funds transfer systems and the variety of approaches adopted by different countries. This is an important contribution to our work on enhancing the integrity of the international financial system—a goal to which both the International Monetary Fund and the World Bank are jointly committed.

I very much welcome the sharing of the authors' description of the challenges, findings, and recommendations with a broader audience. I also hope the pragmatic approach of the authors would contribute to developing a better understanding of these systems and enrich the debate among interested parties.

Eduardo Aninat
Deputy Managing Director
International Monetary Fund

Preface

This paper was prepared by an International Monetary Fund–World Bank staff team comprising Mohammed El Qorchi (IMF, Monetary and Financial Systems Department, head of the team), Samuel Munzele Maimbo (World Bank), and John F. Wilson (IMF, Middle Eastern Department). The research team members visited Germany (Bonn), Pakistan (Karachi), the Philippines (Manila), Saudi Arabia (Riyadh), the United Arab Emirates (Abu Dhabi and Dubai), and the United Kingdom (London). On return, team members continued their discussions with the relevant parties. Later, some team members visited Afghanistan (Kabul, Herat, and Jalalabad) and participated in international conferences on informal remittance systems in Abu Dhabi (May 2002), Oaxaca (September 2002), and London (January 2003), among others.

The authors note that the paper benefited from the review and comments of many colleagues, including Stefan Ingves, V. Sundararajan, Barry Johnston, Tomás Baliño, Patricia Brenner, Zubair Iqbal, Peter Stella (all IMF); Cesare Calari, Marilou Uy, Margery Waxman, Joseph Del Mar Pernia, Simon Bell, Ismail Radwan (all World Bank); and Professor Nikos Passas. The authors also wish to thank Eduardo Aninat, Jeffrey Goldstein, Executive Directors, and staff of several IMF and World Bank departments for their insightful comments and suggestions. The authors are indebted to Steven Kennedy, Natalie Baumer, Oriana Bolvaran, Margarita Aguilar, Mary Wilson, Tsegereda Mulatu, Sarah Guymont, and Baerbel Bernhardt for their assistance and to Archana Kumar of IMF's External Relations Department for editing the Occasional Paper and coordinating its production.

1 Overview

Since the September 11, 2001, terrorist attacks in the United States, there has been renewed public interest in informal funds transfer (IFT) systems. Press coverage, which often focused on the putative connection between the IFT systems and terrorist financing activities, helped to increase the level of official concern about IFT systems' potential susceptibility to financial abuse. Some national financial regulators began examining existing regulations and, in some cases, designing, developing, and implementing new financial sector policies, including those that address IFT systems.[1] Such actions led to a need to better understand the historical context within which IFT systems have evolved, the operational features that make the systems attractive, the fiscal and monetary implications for remitting and recipient countries, and the regulatory and supervisory responses to its current usage.

Background, Definitions, and Recommendations

This paper presents the findings, analyses, and conclusions of a study on the operational characteristics of informal "hawala," which is used predominantly in the Middle East and South Asia. Recognizing that in some of the countries in these regions, the term "hawala" is also used to refer to money transfers in the formal financial sector, the study used the term "informal hawala system" to refer broadly to money transfers that occur in the absence of, or are parallel to, formal banking sector channels. Specifically, the study examined the (1) historical and socioeconomic context within which hawala has evolved; (2) operational features that make the system attractive for both legitimate and illegitimate uses; (3) fiscal and monetary implica-

tions for informal-hawala-remitting and hawala-recipient countries; and (4) current regulatory and supervisory responses.

Recognizing that the reasons for the development of informal financial systems are many and varied, the study conducted qualitative and quantitative analyses to describe the informal hawala system and reach conclusions about its practice. The key themes of the paper are as follows:

Historical perspective. Despite the different terminology ascribed to IFT systems—fei-ch'ien (China), hui kuan (Hong Kong), hundi (India), hawala (Middle East), padala[2] (Philippines), and phei kwan (Thailand)—their initial growth was primarily rooted in facilitating trade between distant regions at a time when conventional banking instruments were either absent or weak.

Operational characteristics. At present, the operational characteristics ascribed to IFT mechanisms, namely, speed, lower transactions costs, cultural convenience, versatility, and potential anonymity, contribute to their widespread legal and illegal use.

Linkages with formal sector. Generally, the growth of IFT systems seems to be negatively correlated with the level of development of the formal financial sector. Hawala-type operations appear to have prospered in countries with inefficient financial institutions and restrictive financial policies. However, in cases where the user's intent is of an illegal or criminal nature, he or she will use informal financial systems irrespective of the level of financial sector development.

IFTs have important implications for designing and implementing monetary, fiscal, and financial sector regulatory and supervisory policies. Drawing on the experience of selected countries in Asia, Europe, and the Middle East, the study found that

- IFTs reduce the reliability of statistical information available to policymakers. This effec-

---

[1]In October 2001, the Financial Action Task Force on Money Laundering (FATF) agreed to adopting "Special Recommendations on Terrorist Financing," which included extending anti-money-laundering requirements to alternative remittance systems. Report available via the Internet: http://www1.oecd.org/fatf/40RecsTF_entm.

[2]Although often applied to informal fund transfers, the term "padala" can also refer to formal transfers. It is a generic word, which means "to send" anything. Derivations of the word can be applied to transfers through a courier, a bank, a relative, or door-to-door transactions.

tively limits the significance of economic data by underestimating the factors that affect certain economic aggregates, including national accounts.

- IFT transactions can affect the composition of broad money and thus have indirect effects on monetary policy.

- IFT transactions may influence exchange rate operations because they can affect the supply and demand for foreign currency. Whereas informal hawala and other IFT transactions are conceptually a part of national balance of payments (BOP) accounts, accurate compilation is highly unlikely. Published BOP accounts contain little numerical—and certainly no identifiable—traces of this system and, thus, their consequences are difficult to explore.

- IFT systems have negative fiscal implications for both remitting and receiving countries. Since informal funds transfers are conducted outside the formal banking system activity, they are not subject to taxes on income and services. Like any underground economic activity, IFT systems also entail a loss of business for the formal financial sector and thereby of potential government income.

Estimating the size of hawala and other similar transactions cannot be undertaken with any reliability. Despite the difficulty of this task, certain judgments can be made about the possible dimensions of hawala, and some approaches to quantification can give indicative results. Using a select sample of 15 countries, a simulation model in the paper suggests that informal transfers declined over time in those countries that liberalized their financial systems. The use of IFTs for criminal purposes is not taken into consideration in the simulation.

Individual country regulatory and supervisory responses to this phenomenon have been varied. Overall, the study found distinct differences in the regulatory and supervisory responses to the IFT systems between "recipient" and "remitting" countries. In recipient countries, concerns over foreign exchange regimes, the quality of the formal financial sector, and the level of political stability have been important influences on the regulatory attitude toward the systems. However, remitting countries generally have fairly liberal foreign exchange policies and mature financial sectors. The key issue in these countries is the potential abuse of IFT systems by criminals. In the recipient countries, the regulatory response has varied from outright prohibition to benign neglect. In the remitting countries, recent regulatory measures include registration or licensing and customer-reporting and record-keeping requirements.

In the wake of the recently heightened concerns that money launderers and terrorist groups use informal transfer systems, the number of national and international regulatory initiatives to license or regulate IFT activities has increased. Many countries consider benign neglect of the IFT industry as no longer an acceptable policy option. The potential anonymity that characterizes these systems is believed to present risks of money laundering and terrorist financing and therefore needs to be addressed. As national authorities develop and implement enhanced regulatory and supervisory frameworks, the paper

- *Encourages* the following two-pronged approach toward regulation in the context of long-term financial sector development.

  —In countries where an informal hawala system exists alongside a well-functioning conventional banking sector, it is recommended that hawala dealers be registered and keep adequate records in line with the Financial Action Task Force (FATF) recommendations. Efforts should be made to improve the level of transparency in these systems by bringing them closer to the formal financial sector without altering their specific nature. In conflict-torn countries without a functioning banking system, requirements beyond basic registration may not be feasible because of inadequate supervisory capacity.

  —Simultaneously, the regulatory response should address weaknesses that may exist in the formal sector. The formal and informal financial systems tend to benefit from each other's deficiencies. Policymakers should address economic and structural weaknesses that encourage transactions outside the formal financial systems as well as the weaknesses in the formal financial sector itself.

- *Emphasizes* that prescribing regulations alone will not ensure compliance. Regulators need to possess the appropriate supervisory capacity to enforce the regulations, and there need to be incentives to comply with the regulations. Compliance is likely to be weaker where there are major restrictions on transactions through the formal financial system.

- *Cautions* that the application of international standards needs to pay due regard to specific domestic circumstances and legal systems.

- *Concludes* that policymakers should acknowledge the existence of practical reasons, from the customer's point of view, for resorting to these methods rather than to formal banks for international payment purposes. As long as such reasons exist, the hawala and other IFT systems will continue to operate, and thus addressing these systems will require a broader response, including well-conceived economic policies and financial reforms, a well-developed and efficient payments system, and effective regulatory and supervisory frameworks.

Implications for Work of the World Bank and the IMF

Regarding the possible implications of IFT for the work of the World Bank and the IMF, missions may need to survey or compile information on the importance of these systems and on regulations governing them in various countries. This objective could be achieved as part of Fund surveillance work, to the extent that relevant macroeconomic issues arise,[3] conducted in the context of the Bank-Fund Financial Sector Assessment Program (FSAP), or on fact-finding or technical assistance missions. The Bank and the Fund missions could also advise authorities on how to upgrade and enhance regulatory frameworks in the area of IFT systems, allowing countries to benefit from experiences developed elsewhere. The Bank and the IMF advice in this respect would need to take into consideration the reasons underlying the development of IFTs and the specific circumstances of the member countries.

The Bank and the Fund would also review compliance of IFT systems with anti–money laundering and combating the financing of terrorism (AML/CFT) standards in the context of AML/CFT assessments, where IFT systems are considered macrorelevant or pose a serious AML/CFT risk.

At the same time, the World Bank and the IMF technical advice should focus on the developmental benefits of financial reforms and liberalization. In this respect, technical assistance would aim at strengthening payment systems, enhancing competitiveness of formal sectors in the area of funds transfer, and disseminating lessons learned from experiences in countries that succeeded in increasing the share of the formal sector in remittance business. It could emphasize the need to reduce the cost, improve the speed, and simplify the procedures of the formal funds transfer system. In countries with impediments to establishing formal money changers or opening bank branches for fund remittances, technical assistance could be aimed at how best to phase out these hurdles and provide advice on how to design an adequate legal and regulatory framework.

There is increasing recognition that remittances from migrant workers are very important to both the national economy of developing countries and the individual households as a means to escape poverty. Therefore, while remittance systems have recently come under close scrutiny as part of the international efforts to counteract crime financing, there is need to ensure that tighter controls do not negatively affect the availability and the cost of these services for the poor. Better regulation and transparency, improved technology, and greater outreach to rural areas offer big developmental gains. There is increasing demand from donors to draw together emerging knowledge and best practices on remittances; define strategic priorities; and strengthen collaboration between governments, banks, nonbank financial institutions, and nongovernmental organizations (NGOs) to realize these benefits.[4]

---

[3]As indicated in the 2002 IMF paper, "Biennial Review of the Implementation of the Fund's Surveillance and of the 1977 Surveillance Decision—Overview," for surveillance to be effective, individual Article IV consultations need to retain a clear focus on the key issues in each country. The paper is available via the Internet: www.imf.org/external/np/pdr/surv/2002/031302.pdf.

---

[4]In this context, an international conference on remittances, organized by the World Bank and the U.K. Department for International Development, is planned for September 2003.

II Introduction

This study responds to the growing interest in the operational characteristics and economic and regulatory implications of IFT systems. It contributes to the limited analytical literature on financial remittance mechanisms operating outside the conventional banking sector. It draws on the experience of a select sample of countries known to rely on the informal hawala system and reports on the (1) historical context within which the hawala has evolved; (2) operational features that make the system's use attractive for both legitimate and illegitimate purposes; (3) fiscal and monetary implications for hawala-remitting and hawala-recipient countries; and (4) regulatory and supervisory responses. Although quantification of hawala remittances is subject to great uncertainty, this study also attempts to show, through a simulation, how this system can be quantified in 15 countries that are likely recipients of informal remittances.

This paper is primarily based on the results of fact-finding visits to six countries. During these visits research team members conducted discussions with government authorities, academics, and private sector representatives, such as bankers and money changers, who have operational knowledge of hawala and similar systems. The team members visited Germany (Bonn), Pakistan (Karachi), the Philippines (Manila), Saudi Arabia (Riyadh), the United Arab Emirates (Abu Dhabi and Dubai), and the United Kingdom (London), and on return they continued their discussions with the relevant parties. Later, some team members visited Afghanistan (Kabul, Herat, and Jalalabad) and participated in an International Conference on Hawala in Abu Dhabi in May 2002 and other seminars.[5]

This paper does not provide a comprehensive study of the different types of informal funds transfer systems operating in the world today. Rather, by focusing on one—the informal hawala system—it provides an analytical framework for understanding the incentives for using nonbanking channels to transfer funds and the possible economic, legal, and regulatory challenges presented by these channels. The paper describes the system's modern uses, settlement procedures, and legal and regulatory aspects. The description is based on its underlying features, which are similar to those of the other informal remittance systems—speed, lower transaction costs, cultural convenience, versatility, and the potential for anonymity.

Informal hawala transactions cannot be reliably quantified or their global volume accurately estimated. The required documentation and statistics for this kind of analysis are neither readily available nor accessible. The model used in this paper is therefore a simulation, not an "estimation," model. It merely identifies the black market premium on exchange rates as a key factor in the economic incentives for remitters to use the hawala channel rather than a sanctioned, official channel for purposes of sending funds to the home country. Other factors, such as cultural norms and costs of the official channel, play a key role, but they cannot be easily quantified for simulation.

The results of the model presented in this paper should be analyzed carefully because they just illustrate a simulation model based on selected parameters and assumptions. Therefore, there remains tremendous scope for further research in the area of (1) the developmental importance of migrant worker remittances for developing countries, (2) the merits of the different models of regulation, (3) the appropriate model and variables for quantifying the volume of informal hawala transactions, and so on.

This paper is divided into seven sections. Section III defines key terms and outlines the key operational characteristics of informal hawala transactions for analytical purposes. Section IV discusses the historical context within which IFT systems have evolved and describes their modern-day legitimate and illegitimate uses. The economic analysis

---

[5]These included seminars organized by the U.S. Department of Treasury's Financial Crimes Enforcement Network in Washington, May 2002; Oaxaca, September 2002; and by the U.K. government in London, January 2003.

in Section V commences with a review of the settlement process used by hawala operators. This often-neglected aspect of recent studies of informal financial systems has significant implications for making economic policy and establishing effective regulatory and supervisory practices, which are discussed in Section VI. The conclusions are presented in Section VII.

III   Features of the Informal Hawala System

Different terms are used to describe informal funds transfer systems, including "alternative remittance systems," "underground banking," "ethnic banking," and "informal value transfer system." This study uses the term "informal funds transfer systems" for four basic reasons. First, in some jurisdictions, these systems are the dominant means by which financial transfers are conducted and therefore cannot be referred to as "alternative remittance systems." Second, in some communities, informal funds transfer service providers operate openly—with or without government recognition; thus, this system cannot be referred to as "underground." Third, the use of these mechanisms is often cross-cultural and multiethnic; thus the term "ethnic banking" is overly restrictive. Fourth, IFT better captures the sense and nature of financial transfers akin to conventional banking that are of primary interest to this discussion.

Definitions and Conceptual Framework

Hawala. In Arabic, "hawala" simply means "transfer." For analytical purposes, the research team designated the term "informal hawala system" to refer broadly to money transfer mechanisms that exist in the absence of, or are parallel to, conventional banking channels. In some countries, commercial banks use the term hawala to refer to formal sector money transfers. The definition of hawala in this paper excludes the use of the term hawala in the formal banking sector.

Hawala transaction. A hawala transaction, as defined in this paper, encompasses financial transfers that are made by principals, or customers, CA and CB located in countries A and B, respectively, through hawala service providers in their respective countries. These providers, designated hawaladars HA and HB, operate outside the formal financial sector, regardless of the use or purpose of the transaction and the country of remittance or destination. Typically, HA receives funds from CA and asks HB to advance the amount to CB in the local currency equivalent.

In a prototype hawala transaction (see Figure 3.1), an expatriate worker (CA) uses a hawaladar (HA) to arrange a remittance to his or her home country. CA makes a payment in dollars or another currency to this intermediary. The intermediary contacts a hawaladar counterpart (HB) in the receiving country, who arranges payment in local currency to the remitter's family or another beneficiary (CB). Figure 3.1 also shows how a hawaladar can use a reverse transaction to facilitate transfer of funds from a family member in country B to a family member in country A. Obviously, some network of family or connections among hawaladars is required to make such a system work on an ongoing large-scale basis.

Table 3.1 shows the simple balance sheet changes resulting from a hawala remittance for the remitter, the recipient, and the intermediaries. The remitter in country A makes a payment, assumed here to be in U.S. dollars, to a hawaladar in the same country, requesting the equivalent value in his home local currency (LC) be delivered to someone, say, his family in country B. At this level of transaction, the remitter pays out dollars and his net worth declines. At the other end, the recipients receive a local currency delivery and their net worth increases accordingly.[6] The requested transaction is set in motion by a communication from the intermediary in country A to the one in B detailing to whom the payment is to be made along with an agreed-upon way by which the recipient can be identified. Clearly, the intermediary in country B needs to have funds available ahead of time, out of which such payments can be made.

At this point, both remitter and recipient have completed their roles in the transaction's sequence. As for the intermediaries, however, the hawaladar in country A (HA) has received funds in trust without making a payment, and the one in country B has made a payment without receiving its countervalue. Both these hawaladars have taken a financial position in the deal, and this is represented in the lower half of Table 3.1. In effect, HB has made a loan to

---

[6]For present purposes, costs and commissions are omitted.

Figure 3.1. Prototype Informal Hawala Transaction

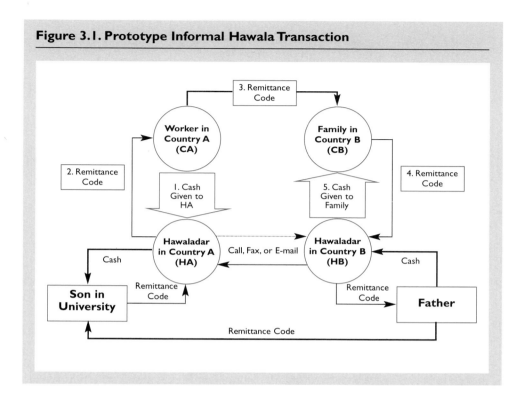

HA, and the transaction needs to be cleared and settled between the intermediaries.

Settlement. After the hawala remittance is completed, HA has a liability to HB, and HB a claim on HA. The principals in the initial transaction do not play any role in the subsequent clearing and balancing of this position. HA and HB can settle their positions in various ways, including simple or complex reverse informal hawala transactions. Such settlements are described in greater detail in Section V. The hawaladars' positions can also be transferred to other intermediaries. These other entities can, by various means, assume and consolidate the initial positions and settle at wholesale or multilateral levels.

Operational Characteristics

The informal hawala system has several characteristics that account for its widespread use. These characteristics include speed, convenience, versatility, and potential for anonymity. The system operates in the informal sector but hawaladars often hold accounts with the banking sector or sometimes use its channels for settlement operations. The system can be used for both legitimate and illegitimate purposes.

Speed. Carrying out hawala transfers between major international cities takes, on average, 6–12

hours. Generally, transfers between countries where the recipient is in a location with a different time zone or where communications are less reliable require 24 hours. Slightly more time may be required for payments in more rural regions or villages where the hawaladar does not have a local office or representative. Telecommunication and information technological advancements have greatly benefited this informal system. Payment orders can now be sent by facsimile, telephone, or e-mail. It must be noted, however, that because the system is based on trust, modern telecommunication is not a prerequisite. In the past, innumerable transactions were carried out by word of mouth, and credit was based on personal note of hand, rather than on documents representing specific goods.

Cost. The direct cost of making funds transfers between major international centers is said to average 2–5 percent.[7] The final quotation depends on the volume of the transaction, the financial relationship between the remitter and the hawaladars, the currency of exchange, the destination of funds, and the

---

[7]In this paper, we consider only the direct transaction cost paid by the customer for the use of the informal hawala system to transfer funds and not the true cost in economic terms. Computing the true economic cost requires more in-depth analysis encompassing several country-specific factors such as the regulatory and tax regime, the level of financial sector development, or other factors such as a war, insolvency, and state ownership.

Table 3.1. Prototype Informal Hawala Remittance Transaction

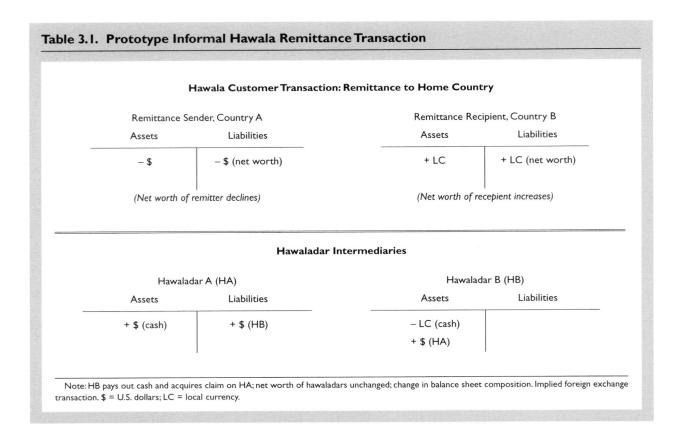

Hawala Customer Transaction: Remittance to Home Country

Remittance Sender, Country A		Remittance Recipient, Country B	
Assets	Liabilities	Assets	Liabilities
– $	– $ (net worth)	+ LC	+ LC (net worth)
(Net worth of remitter declines)		*(Net worth of recepient increases)*	

Hawaladar Intermediaries

Hawaladar A (HA)		Hawaladar B (HB)	
Assets	Liabilities	Assets	Liabilities
+ $ (cash)	+ $ (HB)	– LC (cash)	
		+ $ (HA)	

Note: HB pays out cash and acquires claim on HA; net worth of hawaladars unchanged; change in balance sheet composition. Implied foreign exchange transaction. $ = U.S. dollars; LC = local currency.

negotiating skills of both parties and their understanding of how the market operates. HA can be remunerated by charging a fee or through an exchange rate spread, but often a hawala transaction remains less expensive than payments made through the formal banking sector. The reason is related to hawala's limited overheads and the virtual lack of regulation and taxation. The infrastructure needed by hawaladars to conduct business is simple compared to that of banks involved in international payment transactions or even of money changers. Since hawaladars can operate from either their homes or little shops, or can be accommodated unobtrusively within already existing businesses—from exchange bureaus, brokers, money transmitters, and changers to multibusiness shops such as carpet stores, small supermarkets, travel agencies, and telephone or call shops—few, if any, additional operating costs are incurred by the hawala business. They often need little more than a table, phone, facsimile machine, or—for the most sophisticated—an Internet connection. Unlike banks, little, if any, consideration is given to the commercial and tax aspects of accounting obligations or principles of formal accounting procedures.

Cultural convenience. Absence of language barriers, trust among community members, solidarity among migrants facing the same situation, and cultural considerations have enhanced the development of IFT systems.[8] Limited education levels and illiteracy also pose potential obstacles for expatriate workers, who would not feel comfortable dealing with banks and filling out forms to send money abroad or even open an account. Cultural considerations also apply to family members in the hawala-recipient country and shape social rules and behaviors, including respect for confidentiality and privacy. In many expatriate communities, only men tend to emigrate, leaving their spouses and other family members in the home country. In these communities, conservative and restrictive family traditions sometimes prevail. Women maintain minimal contacts with the "outside world" and do not establish relationships with institutions such as the banks or the post office. A trusted hawaladar, who is known in the village and aware of social codes, would be an acceptable intermediary in such circumstances.

---

[8]This is not to imply that the system is restricted to particular ethnic groups, circles of customers, or retail businesses. This system is used not only by individuals but also often by companies and other institutions.

Versatility. Hawala transactions are highly adaptable to wars, civil unrest, conflicts, economic crisis, weak or nonexistent banking systems, as well as economic sanctions and blockades. The informal hawala system has long existed but only recently gained prominence in conflict-torn regions such as Afghanistan, Iraq, Kosovo, and Somalia. For instance, the formal banking system in Afghanistan is not operational—the six licensed banks in Afghanistan do not provide any commercial banking services. After years of conflict, confidence in the banking system is absent and the remaining banks neither accept deposits nor extend loans. Significantly, banks do not have the capacity to provide international or domestic remittance services. Unless they physically move money around the country, most organizations operating in Afghanistan use the informal financial sector to conduct banking business. Given the security concerns, in the short term, the system has appeared to be the only reliable, convenient, and cost-effective mechanism for fund transfers. Also, hawala transactions are adaptable to different forms of foreign exchange, tax, and other economic regulatory regimes. Their flexibility allows them to be used by persons intent on avoiding or evading taxation. In Guinea, for example, the scarcity of foreign currency in the official market, associated with exchange controls and the expansion of the parallel market for the Guinean franc, boosted a hawala-type system in a parallel market in the 1990s, which enabled people to transfer funds to Europe or the United States within hours. The Nigerian emigrants are reportedly using the informal system to remit funds to their country. Generally, the weakness of local currencies and the related rise in the spread between the official and parallel markets seem to encourage expatriate communities to resort to IFT systems for funds remittance.

Anonymity. Generally, the documentation, if any, used by hawala dealers is inaccessible to third parties. The study found that, in the various countries that the research team visited, there are neither any standard documentary requirements nor accounting methods for conducting business. Except for the slip with the code to be transmitted to the beneficiary, hawaladars do not necessarily need a customer identification document to execute transactions. The recipient needs to only present the code as evidence that he or she is the intended beneficiary of the funds. When some form of customer identification is requested, it is commonly on a voluntary basis. Furthermore, once the transaction is completed, all customer identification documents, codes, or references can be destroyed, except, perhaps, those required for settlement purposes. Consequently, many informal funds transactions leave no audit trail for law enforcement agencies were there to be a need to investigate.

IV   Origin and Modern Uses of IFT Systems

IFT systems are ancient and well rooted in the cultures of various countries. Despite the different terminology ascribed to them—fei-ch'ien (China), hui kuan (Hong Kong), hundi (India), hawala (Middle East), padala (Philippines), and phei kwan (Thailand)—the growth of informal funds transfer systems is primarily entrenched in the monetary facilitation of trade between distant regions. Before the advent of paper money, traders historically used gold and other precious metals for payments. However, insecurity along many trade routes led to developing alternatives that did not require the physical movement of gold and precious metals. This process occurred at different times in the various regions of the world and gave birth to instruments that are similar to, or work on the same basis as, IFT systems.

Historical Perspective

China. The history of funds transfer systems can be dated back to the Tang Dynasty (618–907).[9] With the prospering economic activity during the Tang Dynasty, the need for a system to transfer funds, including tax revenues, became acute, which prompted the emergence of China's ancient remittance system. The creation of the fei-ch'ien (flying money) system seemingly goes back to this time, when business people and government attempted to reduce the inconvenience of carrying currency and facilitate the transfer of funds. Later, by the middle of the Ming Dynasty (1368–1644), with the dwindling circulation of paper money, the government resorted to the remittance system for fund transfers. This practice continued during the Ch'ing Dynasty (1644–1911). In the early part of the eighteenth century, cotton trade played a key role in the development of fund transfers. One of the several networks of cotton dyestuff stores decided to add money transfers to its goods transfer functions. Subsequently, by the end of the century, other dyestuff stores entered the business and created a China-wide network.[10] The fei-ch'ien system, widely used in the tea trade throughout Southeast Asia during this period, was reinvigorated by money changers, gold dealers, and trading companies, who not only wanted to facilitate their trade but also resented using financial intermediaries controlled by the non-Chinese. The system was "exported" to other countries by the Chinese living abroad, and a broad remittance network was established, which covered most of China and even extended to some major cities in Japan, Russia, and Southeast Asia.

South Asia. In the 1950s and 1960s, the main method of payment in the Indian subcontinent was through the hundi (see Box 4.1), chiti,[11] or hawala,[12] which was a draft drawn on a trading associate. Import credit from the "money bazaars" generally took the form of loans against hawalas or hundis. These were simple drafts drawn on correspondent traders in India, the Islamic Republic of Iran, and Pakistan by traders and foreign exchange dealers from the neighboring countries, including Afghanistan. In addition, because currency export from India and Pakistan was illegal, there was a considerable differential between official and hundi exchange rates, which increased the hundi's popularity. Hawala was also used extensively in trade with the Islamic Republic of Iran as well as in domestic trade.[13] Furthermore, after the partition of India and Pakistan in 1947, virtually no payment connected with trade with India and Pakistan was transacted through banks.

---

[9]The authors thank the Chinese authorities for their valuable comments on the history of funds transfer systems in China.

[10]Kaplan (1997).

[11]A piece of paper (e.g., a half banknote) that served as evidence presented by a beneficiary to receive the funds. Although "chiti" came from the Indian language Hindi, it was introduced into China by the English and refers to (along with "chop shop") the Chinese system of alternative remittance.

[12]The term hawala has widely acquired a negative connotation in India. It is associated with illegal payments to politicians and is used by companies for a variety of advances, payments, and transfers. The famous Jain Hawala scandal, involving bribes to politicians, had repercussions throughout the 1990s. This case is recounted in Kapoor (1996).

[13]Fry (1974, p. 240).

Box 4.1. Hundi in India

The hundi is an old system that was used in India before the advent of modern-day banking. The existing literature on this topic contends that the hundi had been in vogue in India from time immemorial. In India, no traces could be found of the existence of paper money in early times, nor is there any reference to negotiable instruments as such in Hindu and Muslim texts. However, bills of exchange have been popular from very remote times. The hundi developed in India with a strong body of rules, usage, and customs, which the legislature or courts of the country could not but recognize and give effect to. In the beginning, the hundis were likely issued by "brokers" for the purpose of debt collection. They took diverse forms, sometimes bills of exchange and other promissory notes, while being sub-ject to local usage. These indigenous bills of exchange acquired such a high level of credibility that to dishonor a hundi was a rare event. They were freely circulated among Indian bankers for financing internal trade and were gradually integrated into the activities of the emerging modern banking system. The redrafted bill tried to reconcile and assimilate the Indian and European Law. The legislature did not abolish the numerous local customs and usages relating to hundis. Because the Indian commercial community was accustomed to using hundis, it was treated as if it were a bill of exchange in some Indian courts. Recently, when political and other corruption scandals erupted, hundi acquired a different perception, which led to its prohibition. Hundi is now illegal in India.

Middle East. In the Arab world, hawala as an IFT system helped to facilitate trade not only within the same areas but also between regions and fiefdoms. Historical accounts refer to instances where hawala-type instruments were widespread in the Middle East centuries ago.[14] Some observers note that hawala developed more than a century ago when immigrant South Asian communities in East Africa and Southeast Asia used it as a means of settling accounts. Others observe that the hawala system dates to Arabic traders who established it as a means of avoiding the endemic robbery of caravans. But the precise antecedents of hawala in the Middle East have not been well documented.

Europe. Operating on similar principles as the modern-day informal hawala, a bill of exchange is an obligation in the form of a payment order addressed to the person responsible for honoring the payment. The bill of exchange requires that a person make payment to another individual on an agreed-upon future date. The bill in its present form was widely used in fourteenth-century Italy. This remittance trade was pioneered by the money exchange dealers who used to display their different moneys on the *banco* (bench) in Italian cities. In Western Europe, the practice of making bills payable to order and transferring them by endorsement originated at the close of the sixteenth or the start of the seventeenth century. The use of bills of exchange later extended into France and then into England, where they contributed to the development of British commerce.[15] Though initially confined to international trade, their use subsequently extended to domestic bills between traders and, finally, to personal transactions.[16] The development of bills of exchange is considered to be one of the cornerstones of the remarkable expansion of banking activity in Europe.

North and South America. In North and South America, the Black Market Peso Exchange (BMPE) is often mentioned in the same context as hawala, with the implication that it is comparable in operation and purposes, often as an important route to launder drug money. The loose association of the BMPE with the hawala remittance system needs careful review, not only because the primary use of the BMPE is money laundering but also because the accounting sequence of the BMPE, as generally portrayed, can differ substantially from that of the informal hawala system as discussed in this paper. Compared with the prototype informal hawala system transaction and settlement process, there are notable differences with some of the transactions attributed to the BMPE. Sometimes what is described as BMPE is a sequence of asset (financial) transactions, starting with a trafficker's hoard of cash that has to be sold leading to those funds being laundered through formal financial institutions, such as commercial banks. In the process, the BMPE may be used to finance the importing of goods for South American traders with limited access to foreign currency. The complete combination of transactions need not necessarily include or exclude the basic fundamental characteristics of the system as detailed in this paper. In cases where the BMPE broker uses both formal and informal funds transfer mechanisms, the similarity between and the relationship of

---

[14]In Arabic, hawala instruments were was also referred to as *Attalaa* (التلا), a bill on which a debtor writes his name and seals it, offering the holder safe movement between regions (Al Allaili, 1978, p. 101).

[15]Aggarwal (1966).

[16]*Goodwin v. Roberts,* 1875, cited in ibid., p. xvi.

the formal system and the informal hawala system may be more tenuous.

Legitimate Uses

Migrant worker remittances. Large migrant-labor communities often find this system particularly suited to their needs.[17] Compared with formal banking channels, the informal hawala system is often not only less expensive but also can be a more accessible and convenient option for the remittance of funds. Also, the service is available 24 hours a day, every day of the year. The network has a wide coverage, which serves far-flung locations, including remote villages in Pakistan or Bangladesh, whereas banks may not handle such a small transaction or reach those remote areas within a reasonable time. Seldom do dealers fail to effect payment.[18] Sometimes, from the remitter's perspective, default risk can be eliminated through the "confirmation-before-payment" process, where the remitter pays the hawala dealer the value of the funds remitted after the recipient has confirmed receipt of the money.

Humanitarian, emergency, and relief aid in conflict-torn countries. Informal systems are particularly well suited and often the only option in countries at war or emerging from war. In cases such as Afghanistan and Somalia, where the formal financial system is not operating, the majority of aid organizations have used the informal financial sector for international or domestic remittance services for humanitarian, emergency, and relief operations. For most organizations, except the larger ones, the cost and logistical capacity required for the physical transfer of cash is too high. Oftentimes, staff members carry cash when flying into the country for operational duties, but the amounts involved are usually small and meant for overhead expenses, not program needs. For program requirements, the informal hawala system may often be the only option.

Personal investments and expenditures. Often, hawala systems can be used to transfer funds for legitimate personal investments and expenditures such as travel, medical care, or college tuition fees. Sometimes, as discussed in the previous section, it is simply a matter of convenience that funds are transferred though the informal channel rather than the banking sector; but hawala transfers are also used to avoid or evade exchange and capital controls and other economic restrictions.

Illegitimate Uses

Circumventing capital and exchange controls. Countries facing shortages of foreign exchange reserves have often imposed capital controls and created tax barriers for imports. Individuals and businesses seek alternative means to make international funds transfers through the reverse hawala route from countries under exchange controls to other, usually more developed, economies, without any documentary requirements. The incentive to use informal mechanisms to externalize funds is even higher if the capital controls exist in a country where there is an exchange rate risk because of political and economic uncertainties.[19]

Customs, excise, and income tax evasion. Importers sometimes resort to making part of payments to an overseas exporter through IFTs, particularly when customs, excise, and income taxes are high. To avoid paying customs duties, importers request the overseas exporter to "underinvoice" the goods. The difference between the actual price and the invoiced amount is then remitted to the overseas exporter through the medium of hawala. Similarly, when a government grants subsidies based on export receipts to encourage exports, exporters could "overinvoice" to maximize their gains.

Smuggling. Recent literature attributes the growth of the present hawala network, in part, to gold trading and smuggling operations in South Asia in the 1960s and 1970s. To avoid gold import restrictions, traders and smugglers used boats to ship gold from places such as the Gulf Cooperation Council (GCC) countries to South Asia. To remit funds back to their countries of origin or purchase more gold, traders and smugglers (importers) found a solution in the growing population of South Asian nationals working in the GCC countries. To settle their liabilities, hawaladars, in Dubai, for instance, would finance gold exports to their counterparts and clients in South Asia. The remitting workers received better rates because hawaladars charged higher fees from smugglers who made substantial profits from the gold trade. Thus, the smuggling activities benefited

---

[17]The legitimacy of informal hawala transactions is subject to national legal frameworks.

[18]In societies where personal honor and family pride play a key role in social relations and status, dishonoring a commitment has dire consequences for a person's reputation, his business, and family.

[19]Hawaladars may be able to avoid capital controls in the short-term without any difficulty in settling their external accounts. However, if these controls persist, hawaladars may experience difficulty in settling their accounts, especially if the volume of funds transfers requires using the formal banking sector. Different settlement mechanisms may have to be devised (see Section V), including the smuggling of physical cash.

Box 4.2. Terrorism Financed by Informal Hawala: A Hypothetical Example

Setting: Robert lives in country A; Michelle lives in country B. They decide to carry out an action in country A.

The operation: Michelle pays a hawaladar $1,000 in country B (HB) to have the equivalent delivered to Robert in country A. HB contacts a hawaladar in country A (HA) via phone or fax to arrange the payment. Robert receives the $1,000 equivalent in short order. Neither HA nor HB is privy to the reasons behind the transaction.

Technical traces: One phone call or fax between HB and HA.

Institutional involvement: None, except, perhaps, HA withdraws $1,000 equivalent from his local account.

Institutional records: None.

International transaction: None.

Effect of money-transfer reporting requirements: Probably none.

---

from, and enhanced, the existing systems of funds transfers used by expatriates in the Middle East, Southeast Asia, the United Kingdom, and even in North America. This network, it is argued, formed the base for the large-scale hawala operations that exist to this day.

Money laundering activities. Both the formal banking sector and the IFT systems are vulnerable to abuse. The number and variety of methods used to launder the proceeds of criminal and illegal activities and finance terrorist acts continue to become more complex with time. The methods are diverse and can employ both banking and nonbanking channels, including exchange bureaus, check-cashing services, insurers, brokers, and nonfinancial traders. The methods through which IFTs and the formal banking sector can contribute to the placing and layering of funds in the money laundering process are similar, although, as discussed below, the informal transfer systems have peculiarities, which make them particularly vulnerable to abuse.

- First, neither system necessarily involves the physical transfer of funds from one jurisdiction to another. Instead, they depend on a series of accounting debits and credits between the accounts of a network of individuals, companies, accountants, lawyers, and intermediaries. The major potential for using an IFT system for money laundering lies in the fact that the proceeds can be moved away from the place where the crime was committed to destinations where the transaction can either appear legitimate or from where it can be later brought back to the

country through a variety of legitimate routes for the integration process.

- Second, in the same way that banking secrecy laws may facilitate money laundering, the potential anonymity of an IFT system can render it susceptible to processing criminal proceeds in ways that disguise their association with criminal activities such as drug trafficking, prostitution, corruption, and tax evasion.

For criminals, laundering money through the formal financial systems in the early stages of the laundering process has the disadvantage of leaving behind a paper trail that can be traced during an investigation by law enforcement agencies. IFT systems, however, can minimize detection risk because they require little or no documentation. In instances where hawaladars maintain records, law enforcements officials cannot generally access them.

Terrorist financing. The anonymous transfer of funds through the IFT systems has also raised concerns about their potential use as a conduit for terrorist funds. Because there is no requirement for identification documents or source of funds, an IFT dealer can initiate or facilitate a multiplicity of transfers, which conceal the ultimate origin of the funds through their network in different jurisdictions. The recipient of funds can use them to carry out a terrorist act. Once the transaction is completed, all customer identification documents, codes, or references are most likely destroyed, except, perhaps, those required for settlement purposes. Box 4.2 illustrates how, for example, an IFT system can be used for terrorist financing.

V Economic Analysis of Informal Hawala Transactions

Assertions that hawala "sends money without sending money" are misleading. Many discussions of remittances through the informal funds transfer systems give the impression that this kind of transaction is very different from making international payments through established institutions, such as banks or money exchanges.[20] It is as if in informal hawala transactions, "money" simply submerges on one side of a border and pops up in a village on the other side, with no further complications, and in a manner unlike that of any other kind of financial transaction. Table 5.1 gives a summary overview of how value is transferred in various kinds of channels.

In fact, as illustrated in Table 5.1, the modalities of hawala transmission are similar to other kinds of international payments, including those that go through formal banking systems. The accounting details are also similar and are discussed in Appendix I. The principal difference is that hawala and other informal transactions pass through unregulated channels. The funds involved may not find their way through a banking institution until later in the process, and sometimes they may never get into a banking channel at all. Except in cases where hard cash is actually sent or carried across a border, remittance and payment systems generally rely on transmission of a payment order that is based on receipt of some funds at the remitting end of the transaction. Actual payment is made to the beneficiary out of balances at the receiving end; settlement follows or, in cases where there are no exchange control issues, institutional accounts can be debited/credited congruently. The point of this example is to demonstrate that payment modalities around the world are similar in terms of mechanics; the main difference among them is selection of formal or informal channels. Consequently, the monetary, fiscal, and legal implications of informal funds transfer systems rest primarily in the unrecorded nature of the settlement procedures between hawala dealers.

---

[20]For example, "Hawala works by transferring money without actually moving it. In fact 'money transfer without money movement' is a definition of hawala that was used, successfully, in a hawala money laundering case" (Jost and Sandhu, 2000, p. 2).

Settlement Procedures

Returning to the prototype hawala remittance discussed earlier, there are numerous means by which outstanding positions can be settled. Below, we briefly outline some commonly used methods, such as simple reverse informal hawala transactions, bilateral and multilateral financial settlements, bilateral and multilateral trade, smuggling, purchase of international services, and other international asset transactions including capital flight. We also consider the possibility of more complex settlement procedures involving higher level intermediaries in the financing chain. Although the settlement aspect of informal hawala transactions is elusive, there are various possible designs, and some observations can be made about the mechanisms. Detailed accounting steps involved in the principal settlement mechanisms can be found in Appendix I.

Simple reverse transaction. The most obvious form of settlement for hawala accounts would seem to be simple "reverse hawala," that is, a remittance or payment going in the opposite direction (see Appendix Table A1.1). While it is possible, the likelihood of account balancing through a "reverse hawala" is still fairly small, not only because of the low probability that hawala remittances from country B to country A would pass through the same hawaladars but also, more important, because aggregate remittance flows are highly asymmetrical among countries. Some countries, such as those with large numbers of migrant workers, are natural net sources of remittances; countries that are sources of emigration are natural net recipients of such remittances. Thus, the GCC countries, Europe, and even the United States will have large outflows of private transfers, while South Asian and some Latin American countries will probably have substantial net inflows. It would, therefore, seem mathematically difficult for a significant fraction of hawala activity to be "settled" through simple or bilateral reverse transactions.

Complex reverse transaction. Hawaladars could use more complicated reverse informal hawala transactions for settlement purposes. In a country subject

Table 5.1. Types of International Funds Transfer Systems

Type of Transfer	Transfer Mechanism	Money Sent?
Formal channels		
Cash[1,2]	Cash carried across the border	Yes
Exchange houses[3]	Payment instruction transmitted	No
Money remitters[3]	Payment instruction transmitted	No
Commercial banks[3]	Payment instruction transmitted	No
Informal channels[2]		
Hawala	"Transfer" payment instruction transmitted	No
Hundi[4]	"Collect" payment instruction transmitted	No
Fei Ch'ien	"Flying money" payment instruction transmitted	No
Chits and chops[5]	"Notes, seals" payment instruction transmitted	No

[1]Legitimate in some cases; not usually accounted for as remittances in BOP accounts.

[2]Unlikely to be captured in BOP accounts; unlikely to have noticeable effect on monetary accounts.

[3]Licenses of registered institutions usually require them to deal only with licensed institutions (e.g., banks) in counterpart countries. Ensuing balances are usually settled through correspondent banking connections.

[4]South Asian name for hawala; similar transfer mechanism.

[5]"A client who wants to send funds overseas contacts someone at a store who will take the cash, make an entry in a ledger book, and then telephone another business in the city of the recipient. The client will at the same time contact the recipients to let them know where to go and collect the money in local currency. The recipients may have to show a chit or token" (Passas, 2000, p. 17).

to exchange or capital controls, HB could receive local currency from an individual interested in having funds abroad (country C). If the initial transaction is not settled, HB might ask HA for assistance. HA would recommend another hawaladar in country C (HC), either because they are correspondents or because an open position between them had remained unsettled from an earlier transaction. Alternatively, HA can instruct HC to make funds available to any beneficiary in country C. In other cases, HB would deal directly with HC and instruct HA to settle the transaction, which would also clear the initial position. Complex or multilateral reverse transactions assume the existence of a large network of hawaladars across countries.

Bilateral financial settlement. Conceptually, the simplest manner of settling a hawala transaction is for HA to make payment directly to HB, or into HB's bank account (see Appendix Table A1.2). In this way, HA's and HB's balance sheets are restored to the status quo ante and accounts are squared. This kind of settlement may well take place on occasion, but probably not in HB's home country account. Bilateral financial settlement through HB's home country account implies an explicit foreign exchange transaction such as the purchase by HA of HB's local currency counterpart to the hawala amount, or an absence of restrictions in country B on residents' holding of foreign currency accounts. In such a case, HA could simply deposit

to HB's credit the foreign currency amount received from the initial customer.

Multilateral financial settlement. The absence of constraints permitting simple financial settlements is, however, an unlikely configuration for countries that are hawala recipients, so settlements in this form will probably not transpire, at least in the variant just described. A more likely scenario might be bilateral financial settlement using third country accounts. That is, HA can settle his obligation to HB with a deposit to some account maintained by HB in country C, which is presumed to be a country, like A, that accepts convertible currency transactions. Obviously, this kind of settlement entails a form of capital export/capital flight on the part of HB, who now acquires a foreign-currency-denominated balance outside country B, as recompense for a payment made in his local currency on instructions received from HA. Since no actual foreign exchange transaction (purchase/sale) has taken place in this sequence of events, the underlying exchange rate remains implicit in the relationship between the hawala remittance and the settlement amounts. "Financial settlement" in a third country illustrates (1) how connected international transactions can take place in circuitous fashion and (2) the possible connection of the hawala channel to "capital flight" in recipient countries with exchange controls.

Bilateral trade. An obvious possible use of HB's balances in a foreign bank, if settled with HA, might be to finance imports to country B (see Appendix Table A1.3). Another possibility would be for HA to pay the costs of these goods. Again, there are various possibilities. In essence, HA clears his obligation to HB by exporting goods to HB, and the latter satisfies his claim by accepting goods rather than cash. The simplest variant of settlement via trade would be the export of goods from country A to country B. This can be envisioned as a trade flow directly between HA and HB (who may also be in the import-export business), or, more generally, it can be envisioned as trade between third parties in countries A and B, that is, individuals/groups to whom the original hawaladars have transferred their bilateral claims and obligations.

Multilateral trade. With this consideration, the potential complexity and variety of "hawala settlement" comes into even sharper perspective. It is also possible to write plausible scenarios in which exports originate from a third country. Thus, the settlement counterparty to a hawala remittance (or various transactions) from the Middle East to a South Asian country could well be exports to that country from Europe that are paid for by the hawaladar in the Middle East. A second scenario might involve exports from a third country to a location that is not country B, that is, HB has transferred his claim to an associate in another country. This seems likely when HB has a liability to a hawaladar who is located in that other country. Cases like these, obviously, will entail a chain of transactions in which the original informal remittance is likely to be totally invisible.

Misstatement of trade values. A related type of trade settlement would not be outright smuggling but over- or underinvoicing of exports and imports. This would have a similar, if slower, effect in "reimbursing" hawaladar claimants for sums advanced to recipients of remittances. Here the potential complication is not concealing imports entirely, but rather letting them be recorded at an understated value. In the case of undervaluation, of course, the importer in country B may also benefit from reduced tariff payments, a factor that in theory can also be taken into account between HB and HA as they work out such transactions.

Smuggling. In considering "trade settlement" of hawala, the possibility of smuggling into country B looms as another variant. After a typical hawala remittance, HB would be "entitled" to a quantity of merchandise, which is equivalent to the value of the hawala payment made, at the implicit exchange rate. A traditional answer to this problem has been the smuggling of merchandise into country B, which "clears the books" without the complication of declaring the trade flow or associated payments. The classic, often-cited instance of smuggling as the "settlement counterpart" to hawala is the gold trade, say,

between the GCC countries and South Asia. Given the labor/migrant relations between South Asia and the GCC countries, the predominant remittance flows, the currency rules, the popular desire for gold, combined with India's (since discarded) longtime ban on private gold imports, it is hardly surprising that gold smuggling across the Indian Ocean was a busy activity that fit into the hawala context as a natural clearing and settlement mechanism.

International services. Another acknowledged form of clearing/settlement for informal hawala transactions is the provision of travel or other international services to HB or other residents of country B, financed by HA or associated consolidators (see Appendix Table A1.4). In effect, residents of country B who want to travel or purchase services abroad, for medical or educational purposes, for example, but who might be constrained by foreign exchange rationing imposed by the authorities, may have an option to "purchase" these services with local currency from HB or local consolidators. As explained above, reverse hawala is a well-suited channel to conduct these transactions. HB himself is the potential consumer of international services, and this transaction is paid for by HA, which liquidates both accounts.[21]

International investment transactions and capital flight. This is similar to HB acquiring a foreign bank deposit, but with a wider menu (see Appendix Table A1.5). In such a case, HB or his financial correspondent could acquire other foreign assets (financial paper such as bonds or stocks, real estate, and the like) in exchange for a claim on HA. HA, for his part, would likely purchase the desired assets in the name of HB or HB's associate, so as to liquidate the liability. In this scenario, HA's liability is discharged, and HB remains with external financial or real assets over a broad range. In technical terms, HB's external claim on HA is exchanged for a foreign asset of another kind. The procedure described here might well be used in countries where the acquisition of foreign assets is forbidden or restricted to specific types or amounts in an effort to "conserve" foreign exchange or reserve the stock of foreign exchange for sanctioned, official uses. The settlement will indeed offer an interesting channel for entities looking to "flee" the domestic currency and acquire external foreign currency assets. Once again, in the chain of transactions discussed here, none of the

---

[21]An interesting, and plausible, account of bilateral hawala settlements via provision of—or payment for—international services is given by Mr. Rahim Bariek (Bariek Money Transfer) in the U.S. Senate hearings in November 2001 (see U.S. Senate, 2001b). In this case all the participants in the hawala circuit are described as family members.

Figure 5.1. Balance of Payments Entries in Remitting and Recipient Countries

Country A (Remitter)		*Country B (Recipient)*
	Current Account	
Unrequited transfers: (−)		Unrequited transfers: (+)
	Financial Account	
Increase in liabilities: (+)		Increase in assets: (−)

transactors have carried out an open purchase or sale of foreign exchange, but they have operated in separate currencies using an implicit exchange rate between them. From the moment of the initial remittance, at least two of the participants, HA and HB, have assumed international financial positions without going through the official sector. This is unlikely to be a problem for HA, but HB or his client has from the start acquired a cross-border asset, his claim on HA, merely by paying out local currency funds to a beneficiary of the remitter.

Higher level intermediaries. As implied by the potential complexities of the arrangements, settlement of informal remittances is likely to go beyond direct bilateral deals and may well involve several hawaladars located in different countries. It is also plausible that there are higher levels of financial consolidation in the hawala chain, that is, a smaller number of players who each take larger positions than the original intermediaries, HA and HB. Hawaladars who have wide networks and conduct substantial transactions can play this role, as can individuals or entities not engaged in hawala at all. However, neither on-site discussions nor the literature revealed any specific instances where individuals or groups admitted to being consolidators.

Balance of Payments

As illustrated earlier, the accounting and mechanics of the informal hawala system and transfers through other IFT channels are, in many ways, similar to transfers made through banks, exchangehouses, and other entities in the formal sector of the economy. All such transfers are, in theory, part of the balance of payments (BOP) accounts, whether or not "money is actually moved" or a foreign exchange purchase or sale takes place, because the remittance itself is intrinsically paired with an international capital flow that provides the financing. That is, considering the prototype hawala remittance as a whole, the action of the remitter to "send funds" across borders to a beneficiary is enabled by the willingness and

ability of at least two hawaladars to finance this transaction by changing their cross-border asset and liability positions. The hawaladar on the remitter's side receives payment and assumes a cross-border liability, with the agent on the receiving side making payment in exchange for a cross-border asset.

In simple balance of payments terms, the action of making a hawala remittance gives rise, at least in concept, to the following BOP entries for the two countries involved, of which there are a number of components (see Figure 5.1).

The transfer is a debit for the remitting country, offset—indeed, financed—by an increase in liabilities (credit) of the remitter, and the converse obtains for the receiving country. "Net" effects for both countries are zero. Three aspects of this example are useful to keep in mind for understanding the BOP context of such transactions.

First, a hawala remittance is indeed a BOP transaction, not because "money is sent" across borders or there is any recorded purchase or sale of foreign exchange, but because the transaction is intrinsically linked to changes in international assets and liabilities that are the financing counterpart. Thus, a seemingly domestic payment, such as paying cash from one U.K. resident to another, may generate other, cross-border transactions that are all part of a set of BOP flows. If these transactions could be measured and compiled into each country's BOP accounts, they would be visible.

Second, it is intuitively clear that none of the four components of this prototype informal sector transaction is likely to be measured or captured in the BOP accounts of either country involved. The individuals or entities involved are not part of any "reporting universe" that files information with the relevant authorities. This means not only that IFT transactions are not reflected in national BOP accounts but also that they probably will not contribute to errors and omissions, so there is not even an indication that something is missing or badly measured. As suggested by the above discussion, nonzero errors and omission values depend crucially on partial measurement of connected international transactions. In a compact example such as this one, if all the components of the sequence are beyond measurement, there is no trace of errors or omissions at all.[22]

Third, cash movements across borders play no role in hawala remittances nor do they, indeed, in most international remittances.[23] Nothing in the sequence of the hawala transfer, or most of the settlement variants, causes physical cash to move across borders. What "moves" are asset and liability positions, that is, bookkeeping entries of the hawaladar participants and related parties. Indeed, the hawala payments flow—from a remitter to HA (in, say, dollars) and from HB to a recipient (in local currency)—is typically domestic, not cross-border. Of course, if HA clears the liability by paying the cash collected in this transaction into HB's account in some banking system, the currency may find its way back to some other venue, or to the United States, but it is not destined for South Asia. This point is worth bearing in mind because in some countries, notably Pakistan, purchases of cash dollars in the black or parallel market by the authorities are counted as part of hawala remittances in compiling net inward transfers in the balance of payments statistics. In fact, such currency is not part of hawala remittances, and only a fraction of the total is likely to be a part of "current transfers" in a technical sense.[24]

Therefore, the main point to be made with regard to the balance of payments context is that while hawala and other IFT transactions are conceptually a part of national BOP accounts, accurate compilation is highly unlikely. Published BOP accounts probably contain little numerical—and certainly no identifiable—traces of hawala, and, thus, no empirical handle can be grasped to quantify or explore the dimensions and forms of these kinds of transactions.[25] Any attempt at quantification (such as the one we make below) must be based on indirect measurement and heavy use of prior information or parameters in whatever model may be used.

Macroeconomic Implications

Monetary and exchange policy formulation. Because IFT transactions are not reflected in official statistics, the remittance of funds from one country to another is not recorded as an increase in the recipient country's foreign assets or in the remitting country's liabilities. While, on the one hand, the direct impact on the policy options of IFT systems is not obvious, however, its indirect impact on monetary and exchange rate policy choices can be significant. The size of the informal financial sector can grow considerably if the distortions between the official and parallel exchange rate are significant. On the other hand, large-scale hawala or other IFT transactions could exacerbate these distortions by diverting foreign currency away from the banking system and further widening the exchange spread. Such developments could influence the formulation and effectiveness of exchange rate policy. The flight of foreign currency outside the formal banking sector could also lead monetary authorities to change the course of monetary policy. They could, for instance, encourage banks to offer attractive interest rates on both domestic and foreign currency deposits with a view to reducing the amounts of domestic and foreign currency kept outside the banking sector.

Composition of broad money. Because there is no physical movement of cash during informal hawala transactions, only value changes hands; broad money remains unaltered. The beneficiary receives funds in local currency from the hawaladar contact in the recipient country. If the funds come from the hawaladar's cash balances, the direct effect of the transfer of the funds between the concerned parties on broad money is therefore nil. The structure of a monetary survey suggests that almost nothing in hawala remittances or other IFT systems has significant effect on the components of overall national banking assets and liabilities. However, the composition of broad money in a recipient country may be affected by informal hawala transactions. This outcome is related to the cash nature of these transactions. The

---

[22]This is not to say that hawala and other informal financial transactions never give rise to errors and omissions or other effects in BOP accounts. It is certainly possible that some transactions downstream from (and in larger scale than) the initial set described here may be picked up by the BOP compilation systems of one or more of the affected countries. For instance, errors and omissions will be affected when only one side of an operation (such as imports) is recorded by official statistics whereas the financing side is not captured in the data. This depends crucially on both the particular form of the (usually capital) flows and the details of the BOP compilation sources used by national authorities, topics that are beyond the scope of the present discussion.

[23]Physical currency movements are discussed, inter alia, in Wilson (1992).

[24]There are many ways that "cash dollars" can wind up in curb markets in various countries, most of which should be technically classified as capital flows. If an expatriate worker brings cash home and gives it to his family, this could be considered a bona fide remittance. There is, unfortunately, no feasible way to measure boundaries between the different kinds of transactions that can put foreign cash in local markets.

[25]For example, to measure capital flows of nonbank sectors, some countries now use the Bank for International Settlements (BIS) international banking statistics. Hawala transactions "financed" by capital (out) flows directed to foreign bank accounts might affect these numbers, but there is no way to associate variations in such balances with background transactions, of which there are many besides the hawala-related ones.

pool of cash available to hawala in recipient countries (HB) is supplied by individuals or groups in these countries that provide local currency to receive funds from abroad. The monetary effect of these informal transactions, in comparison with official transfers, would be reflected in a decline in deposit accounts (possibly savings and time deposits) in favor of an increase of cash in circulation.[26] Since beneficiaries of remittances are usually in low-income categories and rarely have bank accounts, and considering that those interested in using hawala channel transactions for accumulating assets abroad are usually in higher income groups, these transactions would have an impact on the composition of broad money. The adverse impact of the informal hawala system on the banking sector and the related development of a cash economy could increase the instability of demand for money, limit financial intermediation, and affect monetary transmission mechanisms, restraining thereby the efficiency of monetary policy. The flourishing of a cash economy and the related leakage of money away from the banking system could also constrain the availability of bank resources and push up interest rates in the economy, as banks attempt to attract deposits by offering higher interest rates. The impact on interest rates is likely to be aggravated if the loss of government revenue from hawala-related activities significantly exacerbates the fiscal situation and requires the government to resort to monetary and bank financing.

Private consumption patterns. Remittances, in general, either through the formal or the informal system are reflected in private consumption. Even though some expatriate workers send funds home for investment purposes, such as in real estate, it is generally agreed that remittances are overwhelmingly aimed at covering the basic needs of families in home countries. Hawala transactions initiated from countries with exchange and capital controls tend to reinforce this consumption pattern, since the indirect transfer of funds in the recipient country from wealthy groups to relatives of expatriate blue collar workers through hawaladars tends to favor consumption spending over savings. The wealthy groups may use their savings accounts to provide funds in local currency and in cash to local hawaladars, who would subsequently funnel them to beneficiaries with high propensity to consume.

Foreign exchange operations. In economies structurally in need of foreign currency, the loss of foreign exchange in the formal banking system related to the use of IFT systems has contributed to a "virtual" parallel exchange market where foreign exchange can easily be accessed. Even though the supply of foreign exchange through the IFTs disappears from the official market, the informal supply still finances imports of goods and services and thereby responds at least partially to a potential demand for foreign currency that would otherwise have been expressed in the official market. In some countries, such as Pakistan, the shortage of foreign exchange in the official market has required central banks to purchase foreign exchange from the black markets. Such a move indirectly influences the level and composition of broad money. Purchases from the parallel market entail a "recycling" of foreign currency into the formal sector through increases in central bank foreign assets, but foreign currency would be supplied by foreign correspondents of money changers or other intermediaries.

Fiscal policy. Because they generally operate outside the formal banking system activity and do not pay any taxes, the IFT systems have fiscal implications for both remitting and receiving countries. Moreover, like any underground economic activity, IFT systems also entail a loss of business for the financial sector and thereby reduce government income.

The loss of government revenue occurs in two ways: first, through loss of direct taxes in the form of income and other business taxes. The income and profits of hawaladars are unrecorded and likely to escape taxation. Second, hawaladars do not pay indirect taxes such as VAT and other service taxes. The hawala business of fund transfers is not subject to other kinds of taxes, like the formal sector, such as registration fees, and so on. Under the assumption that the informal hawala system tends to favor basic consumption, government revenue may incur further loss because taxes on these goods are usually lower. However, this possible loss is not just related to IFT systems because transfers through the formal sector would have the same effect. In some cases, government efforts to encourage remittances through formal channels are accompanied by tax exemption or subsidies, which would also affect fiscal balances.

As mentioned earlier, reverse transactions may be intertwined with undeclared domestic and international activities. Related transactions used for settlements, such as smuggling, and under- and overinvoicing in domestic as well as in international transactions, evade tax systems or increase spending (subsidies). By facilitating bogus or irregular import and export transactions, the IFT system can indirectly

---

[26]The mechanism is somewhat similar for money changers and other remitters in the sense that cash is mostly used in official transfers. The difference, however, is that in official transfer transactions, cash usually reintegrates rapidly in the banking system while in the hawala system cash reintegrates in the banking system, if at all, only at a later stage in the process.

have a deleterious impact on the government in the form of lower tax receipts from imports and expropriation of export subsidies. The loss of government income is not directly related to IFTs, but it is inherent in part of smuggling or tax evasion activities. In domestic markets, underinvoicing the value of real estate transactions or any other transaction conducted in the real or financial markets with a view to exporting funds abroad facilitates tax fraud and evasion. The informal nature of the informal hawala system, through reverse transactions, offers a discreet medium to those eager to send their wealth overseas without leaving detectable tracks. It offers a reliable medium that allows capital flight to safe havens and investment abroad without declaring the generated income to tax administration. By providing financing to unrecorded imports, the system indirectly favors the circulation of goods and facilitates import of smuggled goods—such as electronics, gold, and diamonds—contributing, therefore, to the expansion of informal economic activities that avoid tax payments.

Information and economic data. As an underground activity, IFT systems reduce the information available to policymakers, particularly central banks, and limit significantly the meaning of economic data by underestimating the factors that affect economic aggregates, including national accounts. In this regard, they constrain the capacity of economic authorities to have a truthful picture of the status of, and the changes in, economic activity; project its trends; and devise appropriate economic policy responses. This handicap may adversely affect policymaking in all economic areas, especially monetary and fiscal policies.

Quantitative Dimensions

Estimation constraints. It is intuitively clear that IFT transactions cannot be reliably quantified. It would be extremely difficult, if not impossible, to make accurate estimates of either balance sheet or turnover figures in the "money bazaars" or informal activities in general. These difficulties are compounded by the questionable legal status of foreign exchange dealings; the high proportion of smuggling in total foreign trade;[27] and the general lack of available records, especially for statistical or balance of payments purposes. This holds true for both the "remitting" and, especially, the "receiving" sides of the transactions. As discussed earlier, on the receiving side these transactions are sometimes

associated with capital flight motivations and can involve contravention of exchange control regulations, so there is little incentive to keep or make records available.

Approaches to quantification. The limited literature[28] on international transfers and workers' remittances, which recognizes that economic factors—such as black market exchange rates—influence transfer mechanism choices, uses standard data sources and does not actually attempt to quantify amounts sent through informal channels.[29] A few studies have tried to measure informal hawala transactions empirically, mainly through interviews with market participants.[30] Against this background, certain discussions can illustrate the possible dimensions of hawala and refer to some approaches to quantification that can give indicative results. Though conjectural, a few bases on which an effort can be made include

- the ethnic connection and "common knowledge" about the culture or characteristics of populations or countries with a hawala tradition;

- the number, or share, of a country's nationals who are residents or working as expatriates elsewhere, since this will be an important factor in the scale of private remittances;

- the relative inability of banks and other institutions to quickly deliver funds, and the high cost of remittances through sanctioned channels; and

- the existence of an active parallel exchange market. The larger the divergence from the "official" exchange rate, the higher the incentive for all participants to divert their transactions into the informal market. Where parallel markets exist, there has generally been some available measure of the exchange rate divergences, or "black market premium."

---

[28]A good example is Elbadawi and Rocha (1992, p. 9), who note that "there is ample anecdotal evidence that the volume of unofficial remittances is substantial in many countries. . . . There are a variety of informal channels through which the migrant can remit, including triangular operations with family, friends, and middlemen to actually operate outside the home country. Although recourse to informal channels usually involves a cost, the migrant will be willing to incur such costs when there is a large premium between the exchange rates in the black and official markets. . . . The black market premium becomes a central variable in models that focus on the choice of channels of remittances."

[29]An econometric approach to quantification might be considered, but it would also entail heavy assumptions imposed on the estimating functions and results.

[30]At present, the best study known to us is Pohit and Taneja (2000). The authors found "hawala" payments account for up to 15 percent of small-scale trade between India and Bangladesh.

---

[27]Fry (1974, p. 241).

Most of these factors are not easily quantifiable, except in a very rough way. Even good data on the "number of emigrants" from potential recipient countries are generally lacking. What is usually available is a version of international transfers through sanctioned channels and some measure of exchange market conditions, such as official versus private rates.[31] Details of the model specification, steps in the simulation procedure, and the results of the model are given in Appendix II.

---

[31]Franz Pick began this work long ago. See Currency Data and Intelligence's *World Currency Yearbook* (formerly *Pick's Currency Yearbook*), various years.

VI Legal and Regulatory Aspects of the Informal Hawala System

Because of their significance, IFT systems have been the subject of regulatory concern for a very long time. Their recent notoriety has merely rekindled and galvanized this interest. Overall, the study found distinct differences between remitting and recipient countries' government policy toward the informal hawala system. On the one hand, in recipient countries, important influences on the regulatory attitude toward the system have been state policies prohibiting informal financial transfers, the quality of the formal financial sector, and the level of political stability. On the other hand, hawala-remitting countries generally have fairly liberal foreign exchange policies and developed financial sectors. In these countries, the interest in IFT systems primarily stems from concerns about their potential criminal abuse. This section briefly reviews the evolving oversight framework for hawala dealers in some countries in line with changes in government policy. The examples in this section illustrate current practice in a number of countries. The description of one country's approach does not imply that it is the only country pursuing this approach.

Hawala-Recipient Countries

Prohibition of Informal Hawala Transactions

India. Under both the Foreign Exchange Regulation Act (FERA, 1973) and its successor, the Foreign Exchange Management Act (FEMA, 2000), hawala-type transactions have been explicitly prohibited. The number of institutions (notably, "authorized persons," such as banks) permitted to deal in foreign exchange has been closely defined, and the kinds of transactions (travel, medical treatment, acquisition of foreign assets, and so on) permitted for customers have been set forth in regulations that have been frequently revised. The recent FEMA wording specifically addresses hawala-type transactions by prohibiting Indian residents from entering "into any financial transaction in India as consideration for or in association with acquisition or creation or transfer of a right to acquire any asset outside India by any person." Similarly, one of the mandates of the Directorate of Enforcement has been to prevent "remittances of Indians abroad otherwise than through normal banking channels (i.e., through compensatory payments)."

Pakistan. A large number of Pakistanis live abroad and the Pakistani economy has a long history with various forms of capital controls. "Legitimate" remittance channels—on the Pakistani side—have been restricted to licensed banks. Exchange houses are only authorized to carry out currency exchange, not to serve as a channel for net inward remittances. Yet, the official rate for the Pakistani rupee has often been subject to large discounts in the parallel market, which is favorable to various kinds of informal transactions, including hawala. Confidence in Pakistan's economic policies and prospects has fluctuated widely over time, and the stop-go nature of policy changes has sometimes exacerbated the problem. However, since July 2002, a newly promulgated legal and regulatory framework for the transformation of money changers into foreign exchange companies allows money changers a two-year period to register and comply with the relevant prudential rules or capital requirements (see Appendix Table A3.1). After the two-year period, however, money changers will not be allowed to operate unless they register as foreign exchange companies.

Enhancing the Quality of Formal Financial Sector Services

Philippines. Except for the usual business registration requirements with the local authorities, there are no regulatory or supervisory requirements for hawala operators. Although originally regulated and supervised by the central bank, money changers have not been regulated since the economy was liberalized a number of years ago. Instead of directly targeting IFT activity, the Central Bank, through the Bankers Association of the Philippines, has encouraged banks to innovate and replicate the advantages offered by the informal sector. Consequently, banks have started providing such advantages, and continue to do so, for example, door-to-door delivery of cash remitted from abroad. More recently, innovations have included remittance raffles, which allow each remittance to be entered into a raffle offering different prizes ranging from cellular phones to free medical services. Moreover, many banks from the Philippines second their own staff to banks operating in regions where there is a high concentration of Filipino overseas workers. Interaction with their nationals when visiting foreign banks encourages them to remit their savings to the Philippines through the formal sector. However, in light of the new international efforts against money laundering and terrorist financing, money exchange dealers were included in the list of covered institutions mandated to submit certain information about suspicious activities of their customers. They are also required to adhere to the basic principles of the Anti–Money Laundering Act of 2001. In addition, an implementing circular for the licensing and regulation of foreign exchange dealers or money changers is under consideration.

India. The authorities have continued efforts to increase the efficiency and cost-effectiveness of banking services thereby making IFT systems seem less attractive. Massive bank branch expansions in the 1970s and 1980s have also reduced the per branch population. Branches of commercial banks in rural areas have increased access to the formal financial sector. The Reserve Bank of India has also allowed nonbank financial companies to undertake Money Transfer Service Schemes to facilitate swift and easy transfer of personal remittances from abroad to beneficiaries in India. These approved agents can, and do, in turn appoint subagents to ensure wide urban and rural coverage.

Self-Regulation

Afghanistan. The more than 300 registered money exchange dealers in the market have organized themselves into an operational self-regulating market.[32] Estimates of the number of unregistered money exchange dealers in Kabul and around Afghanistan vary widely from 500 to 2,000.[33] The market's equivalent to a conventional Securities and Exchange Commission is an eight-member Execu-

tive Committee that meets regularly to discuss its members' affairs. The committee's executive director and his three assistants direct the activities of the Money Exchange Dealers Association and ensure that each member adheres to the association's unwritten rules of conduct and practices. Membership in the association is voluntary and there are no subscription fees. Each member is entitled to attend the Executive Committee meetings. The open meetings facilitate a learning process for new members.

Hawala-Remitting Countries

In hawala-remitting countries, the regulatory approach varies between registration and licensing, with varying degrees of additional prudential, law enforcement, and anti–money laundering requirements.

Germany. Persons operating remittance services without a license from the German Financial Services Authority (BAFin) are liable to prosecution under Section 54 of the German Banking Act. Fines are imposed for contravention of this rule. Licensed remittance service providers are subject to regular supervision in the same way as other financial service providers. They must comply with the same requirements—fitness and propriety tests, obligation to draw up annual accounts and have them properly audited, regular special audits, and so on.

United Kingdom. Although hawala-type transfers are not in themselves illegal, the authorities' main concern is the need for improvements in registration and record keeping. The recent legislative amendments of late 2001 are aimed primarily at strengthening registration and record keeping by those who participate in hawala-type transactions.[34] As in other hawala-remittance countries, the primary focus is on the potential criminal dimensions of informal payment channels, especially money laundering and terrorist financing. In line with this approach, the administration of laws relating to the informal hawala system is entrusted with H.M. Customs and Excise Department rather than the Financial Services Authority. The U.K. hawala regulatory regime is interesting in two respects.

First, it requires only the registration and not the licensing of hawala operators. H.M. Customs can refuse to register a hawala business only if the applicants provide false information, fail to provide sufficient documentation as required by law, or fail to pay the registration fee. It will not conduct fitness and probity tests of applicants, determine the reasonableness of the applicant's business plan, or assess the

---

[32]Money exchange dealers are required to register their businesses with the Central Bank's International Affairs Department. The registration process includes making a deposit with the Central Bank of 20 million Afghanis (US$526). Thereafter, annual license fees are 1 million Afghanis (US$26).

[33]In the absence of regional records and the open nature of the Kabul money exchange market, these estimates must be viewed as speculative in nature as there is no basis upon which to accept these estimates with any measure of confidence.

---

[34]Statutory Instruments, 2001, No. 3641 of the Anti–Money Laundering Regulations became law on November 9, 2001.

adequacy of the capital proposed for the business. Registration is one of the FATF-recommended options, and the U.K. authorities currently do not see the need for prudential regulation of hawala operators (see Appendix Box A4.2).

Second, it does not prescribe the minimum amount above which a "Suspicious Activity Report" must be prepared. Instead, the United Kingdom operates a suspicion-based system across the regulated financial sector. In its education campaign, H.M. Customs will emphasize that operators bear the responsibility of determining what is suspicious, regardless of the amount, and also be duty bound to keep "sufficient" documentation for adequate customer identification purposes. The only guidance provided is that the operator must be able to "identify customers and record or copy evidence of identity and address."

United States. The government has strengthened the regulatory oversight standards for those remitting informal funds transfers. In the United States, the money remittance trade is well established, but not all participants are required to register with an appropriate authority. In 1993, federal legislation was passed to strengthen record-keeping requirements and integrate the requirements with anti–money laundering requirements. In 2000, the Uniform Money Services Act, promulgated by the National Conference of Commissioners on Uniform State Laws, created licensing provisions for various types of money services businesses. Licensing is set up as a three-tiered structure—if a person is licensed to engage in money transfer services, he or she can also engage in check cashing and currency exchange without having to obtain a separate license for that purpose; if a person is licensed to engage in check cashing, he or she can also engage in currency exchange (but not money transfers); if a person is licensed to engage in currency exchange, he or she may only engage in currency exchange services. In the case of money transmission services, the act specifies the disclosures that must be made in an application for licensure, including information about the licensee (criminal convictions, prior related business history and operations in other states, and material litigation), information about proposed authorized delegates, sample payment instruments, banking information, and any other information reasonably required by the state regulator. After September 11, 2001, the United States passed the USA Patriot Act, which reinforces the responsibility of hawala dealers to register their activities, report suspicious transactions, and be subject to on-site inspections.

Saudi Arabia. Hawala transactions are illegal in Saudi Arabia. The Banking Control Law expressly prohibits unlicensed persons from engaging in any banking business.[35] Any person who disregards this prohibition is liable to be imprisoned for a term not exceeding two years and a fine not exceeding SRls 5,000 for every day the offense continues unabated. Also, the regulations for Money Changing Business restrict money changers to the exchange of currency and purchase and sale of foreign currency, in addition to the purchase and sale of travelers checks and the purchase of bank drafts.[36] However, the Saudi Arabian Monetary Agency may license any money changer to make cash remittances inside and outside the country.[37] When so licensed, money changers are required to maintain, with their correspondents in Saudi Arabia and abroad, or in their offices, full coverage against all outstanding remittances on those correspondents to enable them to settle the value of remittances promptly upon receipt of all orders.[38]

In addition, Saudi Arabia has taken deliberate steps to improve the quality of the services offered by the formal financial sector. To reach out to expatriate communities, banks have launched new activities and services (such as Speed Cash and Tele Dial), which offer competitive services to their customers. Banks have also established branches in areas populated by expatriate communities and reduced charges on remittance-related services. Bank branches have changed their working hours to accommodate their targeted clientele and have started offering more rapid delivery of funds to home countries. Through correspondents in the recipient countries, some banks reportedly undertake door-to-door delivery of funds, using the post office and courier services. Banks have also introduced new financial technology, which has simplified account management and helped maintain loyal customers. On the receiving end, the authorities of some countries have launched campaigns to encourage the use of the formal banking sector by offering incentives to remitters and liberalizing trade and banking transactions. In Pakistan, for instance, the authorities have offered to reimburse the remittance fee to banks and money changers in remitting countries to encourage the channeling of funds through the formal sector.

United Arab Emirates. The U.A.E. has had formal banking-type regulations and supervision practices for nonbank money remitters' operators since the 1980s but has also moved to strengthen its regulatory requirements. Federal Law No. 10 (1980) and subsequent Resolutions No. 31/2/1986 and No.

---

[35]Saudi Arabian Monetary Agency (1994, p. 24). Banking business is defined to include "payment orders, promissory notes and similar other paper of value, foreign exchange transactions and other banking business."

[36]Saudi Arabian Monetary Agency (1981).

[37]Ibid., article 3.

[38]Ibid., article 7.

123/7/92 regarding the regulation of the money changing business in the U.A.E. permit money changers to be licensed as money remitters. The law provides, for example, specific guidance on the documentation required from clients engaged in the funds transfer business (see Appendix Table A3.2). Hawala operators must record details of persons or institutions that transfer an amount—for example, Dh 2,000 or the equivalent—in other currencies. The law requires that only the following original documents be used for customer identification purposes: (1) passport, (2) U.A.E. ID card for U.A.E. nationals, (3) labor card for non-U.A.E. nationals, or (4) driver's license. The operator only needs to record the client's telephone number without the address. In the case of transfers in amounts of less than Dh 2,000, the transferor should be given a receipt without the said details (see Appendix Box A4.1).

The Central Bank of the U.A.E. issued an announcement to hawaladars in the local newspapers on November 4, 2002. To regulate the informal hawala system, the central bank will start registering and issuing a "Simple Certificate" to all hawala brokers in the U.A.E., free of charge. In the announcement, the Central Bank of the U.A.E. assures hawala brokers that their names and details will be kept safe at the Central Bank. Hawala brokers, however, should provide the Central Bank with details of the remitters and beneficiaries who receive transfers from abroad on "simple forms" (available at the Central Bank). They are also required to report suspicious transfers.

The U.A.E. has also been working with the financial sector to improve its service quality. Formal institutions have in some cases attained a high degree of sophistication by adapting financial technology to their customers' needs. Some of them currently offer accounts and electronic cards to their clients, which indicate the remitter ID and a list of beneficiaries with their addresses. These cards are aimed at reducing waiting time, accommodating the remitters, monitoring clients, and encouraging loyalty to the bureaus.

VII   Conclusions

Historically, IFT systems are relatively commonplace. Despite the different terminology ascribed to IFT systems—fei-ch'ien (China), hui kuan (Hong Kong), hundi (India), hawala (Middle East), padala (Philippines), and phei kwan (Thailand)—they developed to provide monetary facilitation of trade between distant regions at a time when conventional banking instruments were either absent or weak. Over time, the operational features of speed, low cost, cultural convenience, versatility, and potential anonymity led to their use for various legal and illegal remittance purposes.

Informal hawala systems have typically thrived in jurisdictions where the formal banking sector is either absent or weak, or where significant distortions exist in payment systems as well as foreign exchange and other financial markets. Generally, except for cases where the purpose of using the informal sector is of an illegal or criminal nature, the growth of informal funds transfer systems seems to be negatively correlated with the level of development and liberalization of the formal financial sector. The study found that these systems are more likely to be prevalent in jurisdictions where the formal banking sector is either virtually absent or not functioning, as is sometimes the case in conflict-torn countries, or does not provide a reliable, cost-effective, and convenient mechanism for the transfer of funds. Where these conditions exist in recipient countries, the system can be used particularly for migrant labor remittances as well as humanitarian, emergency, and relief aid. The attraction to the informal funds transfer systems is also likely to be heightened in countries where inefficient banking institutions operate in an environment of financial policies that include foreign exchange controls.

Illegitimate use of the informal hawala system could occur regardless of the level of development of the financial sector. In cases where the intent of the user is of an illegal or criminal nature, the use of informal financial systems will occur irrespective of the level of financial sector development in the country. While both the formal and informal financial sectors are vulnerable to abuse, the potential anonymity that the system offers the users renders it susceptible to smuggling activities; capital control circumvention; customs, excise, and income tax evasion; money laundering; and terrorist financing operations. These crimes are not new and law enforcement agencies have long been concerned about informal financial mechanisms. For financial sector regulators, however, legislation against financial crimes is a relatively recent phenomenon. In drafting new international standards against financial crimes—registration, licensing, reporting, and record-keeping requirements—financial authorities also need to consider the settlement process between hawala operators and the economic and regulatory implications of hawala-type systems.

The nature of the settlement process of hawala transfers has implications for economic and regulatory policies. Developing appropriate responses to IFT systems requires a clear understanding of both the remittance and settlement mechanisms. Essentially, the accounting details of these informal transactions are similar to those of other international payments, including ones that go through the banking system. Like the informal hawala system, banks do not necessarily move physical cash between branches or correspondent banks when effecting transfers. The main difference between hawala and formal institutions is that the subsequent settlement of hawala accounts usually remains outside formal operating channels that are regulated by national authorities.

Because informal hawala transactions are unrecorded in national accounts and other statistics, the data available to policymakers do not offer a comprehensive and accurate description of the economic and monetary situation of a country and are likely to limit the effectiveness of their policies. A hawala transaction is a balance of payments transaction, not because "money is sent" across borders or there is any recorded purchase or sale of foreign exchange, but because the transaction is intrinsically linked to changes in international assets and liabilities. However, while hawala and other IFT transactions are conceptually part of national BOP accounts, accurate compilation is almost impossible. Nevertheless, even though national authorities are unable to directly maintain records of informal financial transfers, the indirect effects of these transactions on monetary aggregates and operations, as well as on the balance of payments, should be taken into consideration. The system reduces the amount of statistical information available to policymakers on the level of economic activity in the country.

IFT systems have fiscal implications for both remitting and recipient countries. First, hawala operators are typically not taxed. The revenue collection structures required for informal financial business do not exist. Second, the business activities of IFT users are also likely to evade direct and indirect taxation. Third, since the settlement of accounts between hawala operators may include underinvoicing and smuggling of goods and services, the government may also incur losses in its customs and excise duty revenue.

IFT transactions cannot be reliably quantified since accessible records are scarcely available for statistical or BOP purposes. Despite this limitation, certain considerations can be made of the dimensions of IFT transactions, and there are some approaches to quantification that can give indicative results. While these results are rough simulations, they indicate that the monetary and fiscal implications of IFT systems remain significant.

Current regulatory and supervisory practices vary between hawala-recipient and hawala-remitting countries. Overall, the study found distinct differences between the recipient and remitting countries' regulatory and supervisory responses toward the informal hawala system. In recipient countries, concerns over foreign exchange management, capital movements, the quality of the formal financial sector, and the level of political stability have been important influences on the regulatory attitude toward the system. However, hawala-remitting countries generally have fairly liberal foreign exchange policies and developed financial sectors. In these countries, the regulatory and supervisory interest primarily stems from concerns about their potential criminal abuse.

Emerging approaches to international standards need to sufficiently take into account specific domestic circumstances. In the wake of the recently heightened concerns that money launderers and terrorist groups use IFT systems, the number of national and international regulatory initiatives to license or regulate their activities has increased. A number of countries have decided that the potential anonymity characterizing these systems presents risks of money laundering, terrorist financing, and other law enforcement concerns, which preclude a policy of benign neglect. This said, the paper cautions against the application of emerging international standards without due regard to specific domestic circum-

stances. Developing international regulatory and supervisory standards for informal funds transfer systems is a complex process. Differences in the stages of economic development, in general, and the financial sector, in particular, imply that national regulators need to give careful consideration to country-specific circumstances and national legal systems.

Regulators must bear in mind that prescribing regulations alone will not ensure compliance. Regulations are not a panacea for possible abuse of the IFT systems. Specifically, regulators need to possess the appropriate supervisory capacity to enforce the regulations. Also, they must bear in mind that experience shows that restrictive methods will not drive out all businesses involved in unlicensed financial transfer activity from the market. The informal banking system cannot be completely eliminated by means of criminal proceedings and prohibition orders. Policymakers should acknowledge the existence of practical reasons, from the customer's point of view, to resort to these methods rather than formal banks for international payment purposes. As long as such reasons exist, the hawala and other IFT systems will continue to exist.

For purposes of long-term financial sector development, addressing the potential risks of financial abuse and criminal activity requires a two-pronged approach. In the majority of countries where IFT systems exist alongside a functioning conventional banking sector, it is recommended that hawala dealers be registered. In these systems, additional efforts should be made to improve the level of transparency by bringing them closer to the formal financial sector without altering their specific nature. Simultaneously, the regulatory response must address the weaknesses that may exist in the formal sector. The formal and informal financial systems benefit from their mutual deficiencies and each tends to expand when the condition of the other is impaired. High transaction costs; long delays in effecting money remittances; exchange controls; and overly bureaucratic policies and procedures for simple money transfers in the formal system are major incentives for the existence of the informal financial system. To face the challenge, the formal sector should tackle its deficiencies and enhance its competitiveness. In conflict-torn countries with no functioning banking system, imposing requirements beyond basic registration may not be feasible because of the lack of supervisory capacity.

Clearly, the development of various informal funds transfer systems over many years and across many countries points to the important role that these systems can play in the absence of a robust and efficient formal financial sector. However, risks of misuse exist considering the informal nature of these systems, particularly anonymity and lack of records. The ability of the formal financial sector to respond to the legitimate market demand for hawala-type transactions, coupled with prudent regulatory policies for hawala operators, requires sound and sustainable macroeconomic policies, a well-developed payments system, and a healthy financial sector. Notwithstanding the progress apparently made by the formal sector in expanding its activity at the expense of informal activity, these gains are not definitive and can easily be reversed. Poorly functioning financial systems or just the deterioration in financial or macroeconomic conditions could pave the way for greater recourse to informal payment systems. A setback in financial and exchange liberalization or the rise in the exchange spread between official and parallel market exchanges can always induce a greater reliance on IFT activity.

Appendix 1 Types of Settlement for Hawala Intermediaries' Remittances

Table A1.1. Settlement via Reverse Hawala Transaction from Country B to Country A

Reverse Transaction *(Note: Simple exact balancing of initial transactions highly improbable because A to B remittances > B to A remittances.)*

Remittance Sender, Country B

Assets	Liabilities
− LC (cash)	− LC (net worth)

(Net worth of remitter declines)

Remittance Recipient, Country A

Assets	Liabilities
+ $ (cash)	+ $ (net worth)

(Net worth of recepient increases)

Hawaladar B (HB)

Assets	Liabilities
+ $ (cash)	+ $ (HA)

Hawaladar A (HA)

Assets	Liabilities
− LC (cash)	
+ $ (HB)	

Summary of Hawaladar Accounts, Including Reverse Transaction

A to B Remittance

Hawaladar A (HA)

Assets	Liabilities
+ $ (cash)	+ $ (HB)

Hawaladar B (HB)

Assets	Liabilities
− LC (cash)	
+ $ (HA)	

B to A Remittance

Hawaladar A (HA)

Assets	Liabilities
− $ (cash)	
+ $ (HB)	

Hawaladar B (HB)

Assets	Liabilities
+ $ (cash)	+ $ (HA)

Table A1.2. Bilateral Financial Settlement Through Bank in Country A

After Customer Remittance Transaction (see Table 3.1)

Hawaladar A (HA)			Hawaladar B (HB)	
Assets	Liabilities		Assets	Liabilities
− $ (cash)	− $ (HB)		+ $ (BA)	
			− $ (HA)	

Bank A (BA)	
Assets	Liabilities
+ $ (investments)	+ $ (HB)

Note: HA deposits $ in HB's bank account; bank intermediation assumed. Bank A is in country A; exchange controls may impede settlement in country B.

Table A1.3. Bilateral Settlement via Exports to Country B

After Customer Remittance Transaction (see Table 3.1)

Hawaladar A (HA)			Hawaladar B (HB)	
Assets	Liabilities		Assets	Liabilities
− $ (cash)	− $ (HB)		− $ (HA)	
			+ $ (goods)	

Note: HA pays for exports shipped to HB.

Table A1.4. Clearing by Means of International Services for HB Paid for by HA

After Customer Remittance Transaction (see Table 3.1)

Hawaladar A (HA)		Hawaladar B (HB)	
Assets	Liabilities	Assets	Liabilities
– $ (cash)	– $ (HB)	– $ (HA)	– $ (net worth)

Note: HB purchases services from country A; these services paid for by HA, e.g., Pakistan Hajj sponsorship scheme; HB's net worth declines due to services expenditure.

Table A1.5. Clearing by Means of Nonbank Capital Flows

After Customer Remittance Transaction (see Table 3.1)

Hawaladar A (HA)[1]		Hawaladar B (HB)[2]	
Assets	Liabilities	Assets	Liabilities
– $ (cash)[1]	– $ (HB)	– $ (HA)	
		+ $ (shares)	

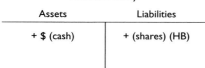

Nonbank Entity[2]	
Assets	Liabilities
+ $ (cash)	+ (shares) (HB)

[1]HA purchases securities, real estate, and so on, in the name of HB, using cash provided by hawala customer.
[2]HB thereby exchanges claim on HA for external portfolio assets.

Box A1.1. Informal Hawala: Levels of Financial Consolidation

Initial Transaction   Remitter and beneficiary transactions effected.
                                 Hawaladars A and B have unsettled balance sheets.

Likelihood of "offsetting" reverse transactions is small.
Country A likely has open capital markets and no currency controls.
Country B may have restricted capital markets and foreign exchange controls.

Consolidation/Aggregation I   Hawaladar A pays amount due to intermediary.
                                  Hawaladar B receives amount due from intermediary.

Higher level "financial" intermediary assumes that balances and amounts increase.
Some empirical evidence of such consolidation.
Intermediaries likely residents/entities in countries A and B.

Consolidation/Aggregation II   Further level(s) of same?

No empirical evidence on number of "consolidation" levels.

Final Settlement   Various permutations.

Goods market: for example, exports/imports; smuggling.
Financial market: accounts with financial institutions.
Miscellaneous international transactions: for example, capital flight; foreign property purchase.

At this point, all parties are cleared and settled.
Likelihood of interaction with formal financial system increases, but hawala background obscure.
Chance of exchange control violations especially in recipient countries.

Appendix II Formulation and Simulation of the Quantification Model

This study used a simple model of hawala remittances constructed for 15 recipient countries that met certain conditions for informal activity, principally (1) appreciable numbers of nonresident nationals, (2) a history of parallel exchange markets with statistically available data on parallel rates, and (3) available statistics on recorded private transfers. For present purposes, the countries selected were Algeria, Bangladesh, Ecuador, El Salvador, Guatemala, India, Indonesia, the Islamic Republic of Iran, Pakistan, the Philippines, Sri Lanka, Sudan, Tanzania, Turkey, and Zimbabwe.[39] In each case the model was applied to cover experience from 1981 to 2000, using officially compiled balance of payments data on inward private transfers and information on parallel market exchange rates, if any, as well as applying the information mentioned above.

The model has the following form for each country examined. The estimated share of hawala remittances in total private transfers is specified as

$$RI/R = a + bB + cB^2 - dB^3,$$

where

RI =	informal remittances/transfers;
R =	total remittances/transfers;
RP =	recorded private transfers in the BOP accounts of each country;
R =	$RI + RP$ (thus, $R = RP/[1-RI/R]$);
B =	"black market premium" (in percent of the official rate) on the currency;
MIN =	intercept ($= a$), that is, minimum share of "hawala" in total remittances (when $B = 0$); and
MAX =	maximum share of informal transfers in total (when B is high).

The model is specified as a cubic function on the assumption that the "hawala share" of total remittances starts at some generally nonzero level if/when $B = 0$, and rises through a certain range of values for B, reaching a peak at some value beyond which RI/R

stabilizes at MAX $(RI/R)^* < 1$. Obviously, this is just a way of saying that hawala transfers cannot exceed total remittances, measured and unmeasured.[40] Assumptions play a large role in this model, because RI cannot be measured directly, and there is no obvious way to assess an error structure in estimation.

To further parameterize the structure, we assume that the inflection point in the curve traced by this model occurs at a value of $B^* = X$, and the maximum value of the hawala share, say $(RI/R)^* = $ MAX, is reached at $Y = 2X$.[41] For values of $B > Y$, it is assumed that RI/R stabilizes at MAX. That is, at least some small portion of total transfers will continue to go through recorded channels, no matter how strong the exchange rate incentive to use unofficial ones.

The contour of this reaction function (that is, RI/R responding to exchange market incentives) seems to be plausible, but the model has to be imposed on available data. Results are obtained by selecting values of the intercept MIN and MAX and X, according to country characteristics and exchange rate experience. For instance, many observers have noted that hawala is deeply entrenched in Pakistan, which suggests the choice value of MIN for Pakistan is well above zero and that of MAX would be high, say around 0.9. That is, the assumptions for Pakistan suggest that hawala remittances may be substantial, even if B is not exceptionally high, and high levels of B may not be needed for hawala remittances to account for a large share of the total.

Another factor to be considered—in choosing "X," in particular—is the exchange rate history of each country in the sample. In some countries there may be parallel markets, but without large or sustained divergences over time between official and black market rates. In others, for example, Algeria or the Islamic Republic of Iran, there is a long history of parallel exchange rates that are far above official rates. This difference in experience raises the analyt-

---

[39]Mexico and others might be included, but in such cases there is no "documented" history of black market exchange rates.

[40]The cubic form suggests a response that first accelerates, and then decelerates, as B rises from zero toward some level at which hawala remittances reach a peak relative to the total.

[41]For $Y = 2X$, the solution value for b equals zero. Other solution values result when $Y = 3X$ or other possible formulations.

Table A2.1. Parameter Values Used in Informal Hawala Estimates

| Country | Intercepts (RI/R) | | Black Market Exchange Rate Premium (B) | |
	MIN[1]	MAX[1]	Inflection (X)[2]	Peak (Y)[2,3]
Algeria	0.2	0.8	100	200
Bangladesh	0.2	0.8	50	100
Ecuador	0.1	0.7	20	40
El Salvador	0.2	0.8	50	100
Guatemala	0.1	0.7	20	40
India	0.1	0.7	15	30
Indonesia	0.2	0.9	20	40
Iran, I.R. of	0.1	0.7	50	100
Pakistan	0.4	0.9	20	40
Philippines	0.05	0.6	10	20
Sri Lanka	0.2	0.9	20	40
Sudan	0.1	0.7	20	40
Tanzania	0.1	0.7	20	40
Turkey	0.1	0.6	10	20
Zimbabwe	0.1	0.7	40	80

[1]Expressed as RI/R.
[2]Black market exchange rate premium over official rate (%).
[3]As implemented, $Y = 2X$.

ical problem of how such countries respond compared to those in which divergences have not been so extreme or protracted. If there is, say, a 100 percent divergence in exchange rates, would a country in which 100 percent might be "below average" have the same degree of hawala remittance activity as a country where this same divergence might be above average? For purposes of this exercise, at least, we assume that "peak levels" of hawala activity occur at *higher* levels of exchange rate divergence (B) in countries with a history of large divergences than for those with a history of small divergences. Thus, peak activity (RI/R) for Algeria, for example, might be reached at a level of B that is well above the maximum for the Philippines.

Figure A2.1 shows the general form of the simulation function. In this figure, MIN = 0.1, MAX = 0.9, $X = 50$, and $Y = 100$.

Parameter choices for the 15 countries included in our sample are shown in Table A2.1.

It is noted again that selected values are judgmental, based on our current understanding of the factors that bear on hawala remittances in each of these countries. While these enable us to obtain estimates, readers are at liberty to experiment with alternative specifications and parameter values based on different assumptions.

Tables A2.2–A2.5 provide an overview of the results of this experiment. These numerical results are only specimens for the 15 included countries, but it is hoped they are illustrative of the potential real world scale of informal payments activities.

Table A2.2 provides a summary overview of the results of this experiment for the entire period.

Table A2.3 displays private current transfers as recorded in national balance of payments statistics and reported to the Fund, usually for publication in *International Financial Statistics*.[42] These series are the data captured by national compilation systems (i.e., those transfers that pass through "sanctioned" channels) but, even there, the measurements are not infallible.[43] Recorded series are merely a rough benchmark to help scale hawala as described above.

Table A2.4 provides time series on approximate black market exchange rate premiums (B), from the sources discussed above and as compiled by the World Bank. This is the second crucial ingredient in making hawala estimates with this particular model. It should be noted, in particular, that the history of black market premiums is quite divergent across countries, and also that in most cases the black market premium tends to decline noticeably from the early 1980s to the late 1990s.[44]

Time-series-simulation results for RI/R (the hawala share) for each of the 15 countries are given in Table A2.5, which can be examined in conjunction with parameter values displayed in Table A2.1.

[42]Not all the countries in this sample compile and report complete BOP data for use in the IMF's *Balance of Payments Statistics Yearbook*.

[43]Note, for instance, anomalies in the transfers/remittances statistics of Pakistan and Philippines.

[44]It is tempting to surmise that Fund advice influenced this result, but it is impossible to know for certain.

Obviously, these results are bounded by MIN and MAX for each country, so somewhat different values could be obtained if an analyst varies these parameters. The lowest intercept for *RI/R* is .05 for the Philippines, for reasons discussed in the text, and the highest value for MAX is 0.9, which applies to Indonesia, Pakistan, and Sri Lanka. However, with the values chosen for *X* and *Y*, there are few instances where these levels are reached.[45] At the same time, given the parameter choices, details in Table A2.5 suggest that the "hawala share" of remittances can be large for many of these countries.

Results. Results of this exercise suggest that the amount of informal remittances around the world can be considerable, especially in view of the fact that only a subset of participant countries is included here. If these results are in any way indicative of actual trends, the global total for informal remittances could amount to billions of dollars. Table A2.2 summarizes total recorded (*RP*) and constructed unrecorded (*RI*) private transfers for each of these countries across the 20-year sample, and the "average" share of unrecorded transfers over this period for each of them. For some of the countries (e.g., Algeria, Bangladesh, the Islamic Republic of Iran, and Pakistan) the results are notably high, and

---

[45]As *X* and *Y* are lowered, of course, it becomes easier to "bump these ceilings" and therefore raise the amount of estimated hawala.

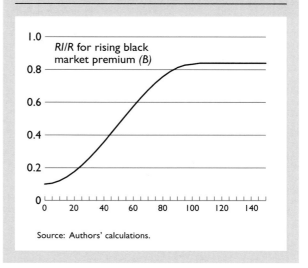

Figure A2.1. Estimating Function for Hawala Share in Total Private Remittances

Source: Authors' calculations.

for a few, especially the Philippines, they are modestly low. India, Ecuador, and Guatemala also fall into a "low" category, or less than 20 percent. This is, of course, reflective of the parameters chosen and could be somewhat raised or lowered with different choices.

Time-series perspectives on these results can be seen in Figures A2.2 and A2.3. The first of these

Table A2.2. Summary of Estimated Private Remittances, 1981–2000
(In billions of dollars)

Country	Total	Recorded	Unrecorded	Share of Unrecorded in Total (percent)
Algeria	53	14	38	73
Bangladesh	84	35	50	59
Ecuador	9	7	2	18
El Salvador	25	15	9	38
Guatemala	8	7	1	16
India	143	120	23	16
Indonesia	16	12	4	23
Iran, I.R. of	98	31	70	68
Pakistan	136	62	75	55
Philippines	55	50	5	9
Sri Lanka	23	14	9	38
Sudan	15	7	9	55
Tanzania	19	8	11	58
Turkey	87	72	14	17
Zimbabwe	6	3	3	44
Total	**776**	**456**	**319**	**41**

Source: Authors' calculations.

Table A2.3. Recorded Private Current Transfers
(In millions of U.S. dollars)

Country	1981	1982	1983	1984	1985	1986	1987	1988	1989	1990	1991	1992	1993	1994	1995	1996	1997	1998	1999	2000
Algeria	513	529	414	350	529	917	628	477	603	400	269	500	1,100	1,400	1,100	900	1,060	1,060	790	790
Bangladesh	933	1,295	1,429	1,266	1,182	1,218	1,503	1,633	1,397	1,614	1,812	1,809	1,952	2,091	2,267	1,913	2,137	2,173	2,501	2,426
Ecuador	35	30	38	25	85	51	135	104	106	119	123	134	318	391	506	616	738	933	1,188	1,437
El Salvador	75	210	154	176	187	252	337	348	438	525	627	853	1,005	1,291	1,393	1,259	1,364	1,534	1,566	1,830
Guatemala	97	66	34	32	21	76	196	228	255	218	277	406	371	456	508	537	629	743	754	911
India	3,026	2,939	3,075	2,789	2,799	2,638	3,034	2,739	3,093	2,853	3,736	4,157	5,375	8,208	8,410	11,350	13,975	10,402	11,958	13,504
Indonesia	250	134	114	167	88	259	257	254	339	418	262	571	537	619	981	937	1,034	1,338	1,914	1,816
Iran, I.R. of	2,000	2,000	2,000	2,000	2,000	2,000	2,000	2,000	2,500	2,500	2,000	1,996	1,500	1,200	800	471	400	500	508	539
Pakistan[1]	2,564	3,175	3,397	3,349	3,095	3,185	2,899	2,760	2,770	2,834	2,890	3,502	2,337	2,919	2,611	2,739	3,981	2,801	3,582	4,188
Philippines[2]	546	810	944	659	694	696	809	874	1,002	1,203	1,521	2,222	2,276	3,009	4,928	4,306	5,742	4,926	6,794	6,050
Sri Lanka	389	451	465	504	469	503	530	564	547	579	645	730	795	882	847	881	967	1,054	1,078	1,166
Sudan	404	132	274	307	369	358	332	334	577	143	128	233	85	120	346	236	439	732	702	651
Tanzania	152	136	128	180	394	501	610	643	682	593	504	650	390	312	370	371	314	427	413	406
Turkey	2,575	2,295	1,806	2,131	2,022	2,030	2,456	2,220	3,574	4,525	5,131	4,075	3,800	3,113	4,512	4,466	4,909	5,860	5,294	5,317
Zimbabwe	142	87	95	193	172	170	221	211	211	204	192	347	271	69	149	126	128	115	122	75

Sources: IMF, International Financial Statistics and Balance of Payments Statistics Yearbook, various years. Some values obtained from IMF Staff Reports or estimated, where missing—Islamic Republic of Iran, pre-1989; Algeria, post-1992 from published country reports; Zimbabwe, 1995ff.

[1]Includes State Bank of Pakistan purchases from the curb market. Fiscal year basis.

[2]Measured as income of Filipino workers overseas, rather than as actual remittances.

Table A2.4. Black Market Exchange Rate Premiums
(In percent of previous period official rate)

Country	1981	1982	1983	1984	1985	1986	1987	1988	1989	1990	1991	1992	1993	1994	1995	1996	1997	1998	1999	2000
Algeria	247	266	330	369	389	246	419	416	358	264	83	300	358	250	175	133	125	150	50	50
Bangladesh	41	41	42	45	130	218	211	272	210	199	136	67	40	30	19	19	11	0	0	0
Ecuador	29	96	64	91	85	0	31	38	16	23	19	10	6	5	4	2	5	11	0	0
El Salvador	84	34	98	100	204	82	100	195	85	36	12	12	18	15	15	10	10	11	0	0
Guatemala	22	25	70	24	45	15	33	28	9	22	14	4	5	4	4	2	2	2	0	0
India	9	13	28	16	17	8	13	14	12	15	18	4	5	5	6	6	3	2	2	2
Indonesia	4	1	0	2	0	11	16	16	3	1	4	26	9	7	5	0	6	11	5	5
Iran, I.R. of	403	379	320	562	557	977	1,576	1,030	1,965	1,965	3,252	3,360	88	100	150	193	186	150	400	200
Pakistan	41	25	30	11	0	1	19	10	0	6	9	8	8	8	6	6	11	25	20	20
Philippines	6	7	50	1	1	2	8	3	4	6	6	1	2	4	7	9	0	0	0	0
Sri Lanka	6	10	38	32	15	3	2	36	25	16	9	10	6	4	1	10	0	11	5	5
Sudan	3	57	54	102	43	122	85	270	344	915	52	95	78	50	25	10	0	11	5	5
Tanzania	193	205	301	287	281	248	139	100	35	50	59	36	9	8	6	4	7	11	5	5
Turkey	20	15	11	1	0	7	8	9	2	1	6	6	4	4	4	0	4	0	4	4
Zimbabwe	53	51	192	80	53	70	50	47	76	37	50	33	19	15	10	7	16	900	400	400

Sources: World Currency Yearbook for 1985, 1990–93; Wood, 1988; Global Development Finance and World Development Indicators for 1996–97. Certain missing values interpolated by the authors.

Table A2.5. Simulated Shares of Informal Hawala in Total Private Transfers
(In percent of total; R = RI + RP)

Country	1981	1982	1983	1984	1985	1986	1987	1988	1989	1990	1991	1992	1993	1994	1995	1996	1997	1998	1999	2000
Algeria	0.80	0.80	0.80	0.80	0.80	0.80	0.80	0.80	0.80	0.80	0.28	0.80	0.80	0.80	0.64	0.43	0.40	0.50	0.23	0.23
Bangladesh	0.28	0.28	0.28	0.30	0.80	0.80	0.80	0.80	0.80	0.80	0.80	0.44	0.27	0.24	0.21	0.21	0.20	0.20	0.20	0.20
Ecuador	0.38	0.70	0.70	0.70	0.70	0.10	0.43	0.62	0.17	0.27	0.20	0.12	0.11	0.11	0.10	0.10	0.11	0.13	0.10	0.10
El Salvador	0.60	0.25	0.77	0.80	0.80	0.57	0.80	0.80	0.61	0.26	0.21	0.21	0.21	0.21	0.21	0.20	0.20	0.20	0.20	0.20
Guatemala	0.25	0.30	0.70	0.28	0.70	0.17	0.47	0.35	0.12	0.25	0.15	0.10	0.11	0.10	0.10	0.10	0.10	0.10	0.10	0.10
India	0.14	0.19	0.60	0.24	0.25	0.13	0.19	0.20	0.17	0.22	0.29	0.11	0.11	0.11	0.12	0.12	0.10	0.10	0.10	0.10
Indonesia	0.20	0.20	0.20	0.20	0.20	0.24	0.28	0.28	0.20	0.20	0.20	0.45	0.22	0.21	0.21	0.20	0.21	0.24	0.21	0.21
Iran, I.R. of	0.70	0.70	0.70	0.70	0.70	0.70	0.70	0.70	0.70	0.70	0.70	0.70	0.54	0.70	0.70	0.70	0.70	0.70	0.70	0.70
Pakistan	0.90	0.56	0.65	0.43	0.40	0.40	0.49	0.42	0.40	0.41	0.42	0.41	0.41	0.41	0.41	0.41	0.43	0.57	0.50	0.50
Philippines	0.09	0.11	0.60	0.05	0.05	0.05	0.12	0.06	0.06	0.08	0.09	0.05	0.05	0.06	0.10	0.14	0.05	0.05	0.05	0.05
Sri Lanka	0.21	0.23	0.83	0.62	0.27	0.20	0.20	0.75	0.43	0.29	0.23	0.23	0.21	0.20	0.20	0.20	0.20	0.20	0.20	0.20
Sudan	0.10	0.70	0.70	0.70	0.70	0.70	0.70	0.70	0.70	0.70	0.70	0.70	0.70	0.70	0.30	0.13	0.10	0.13	0.11	0.11
Tanzania	0.70	0.70	0.70	0.70	0.70	0.70	0.70	0.70	0.54	0.70	0.70	0.58	0.12	0.12	0.11	0.10	0.11	0.13	0.11	0.11
Turkey	0.59	0.36	0.23	0.10	0.10	0.15	0.16	0.18	0.10	0.10	0.13	0.14	0.12	0.11	0.11	0.10	0.12	0.10	0.11	0.11
Zimbabwe	0.33	0.31	0.70	0.70	0.33	0.54	0.30	0.27	0.63	0.20	0.30	0.18	0.12	0.11	0.11	0.10	0.12	0.70	0.70	0.70

Source: Estimates are for RI/R, using methodology described in text.

plots the time series of BOP-recorded private transfers over the period in question. Recorded data start in the vicinity of $15 billion some 20 years ago and rise close to $40 billion by the year 2000. As suggested by earlier comments, if the share of estimated informal hawala transactions has declined somewhat over this period, the share of recorded transfers in the total likely has increased, so that the 20-year rise in recorded transfers may be somewhat stronger than the background increase in total remittances.[46]

Figure A2.3 provides, in bar graph form, a summary of estimated hawala remittances as a share of the total transfers over the sample period. Given the parameters used in the exercise, hawala remittances appear to have receded from some 50–70 percent of totals during the 1980s to somewhere around 20 percent at the end of the 1990s. This reflects changes in the main determinant of informal hawala transactions, the black market exchange rate premium that, for many countries, retreated to near zero during the concluding years of the decade.

Finally, Figure A2.4 expresses the 15-country total of hawala transfers in dollar terms. The results suggest that informal transfers started high, about $35 billion per annum, early in the 1980s, then oscillated in the $15–$20 billion range through the early 1990s, and finally could have declined to around the $10

---

[46]Of course, a decline in the relative share of informal remittances/transfers (*RI*) does not necessarily mean a fall in the absolute values.

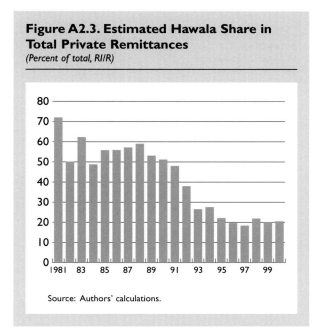

Figure A2.3. Estimated Hawala Share in Total Private Remittances
(Percent of total, RI/R)

Source: Authors' calculations.

billion per annum range late in the sample period. According to our assumptions, this evolution was driven mainly by the "disappearance" of many black market exchange rate premiums for countries included in the investigation. A decline of estimated informal hawala transactions to even lower annual rates is not likely to occur so long as there are ethnic, geographic, cost, or other factors that influence people to stay away from official channels in favor of unofficial ones.

An important consideration is that these empirical results are merely rough simulations that should not be given undue significance in discussions about IFTs. So far as quantification is concerned, there simply is no known means to get authoritative results, and educated guesses are about the best that can be obtained. If these results have any significance at all, they just suggest that the "amount of hawala" can be fairly significant for certain countries that have the economic and cultural conditions that nourish this business, and certainly larger on a world scale than the figures generated by these selected sample cases. More importantly, these results may also suggest that the growth or decline in the use of IFT systems may be negatively correlated to the level of development of the formal financial sector. Hawala-type operations appear to have been more dominant in countries where financial institutions are inefficient or financial policies restrictive. The seemingly downward trend of hawala system usage in the sample countries may be in response to the international move toward more liberal exchange

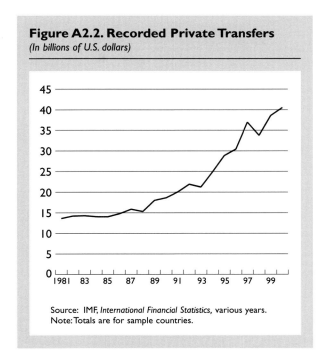

Figure A2.2. Recorded Private Transfers
(In billions of U.S. dollars)

Source: IMF, *International Financial Statistics*, various years.
Note: Totals are for sample countries.

Figure A2.4. Estimated Value of Hawala Transfers
(In billions of U.S. dollars)

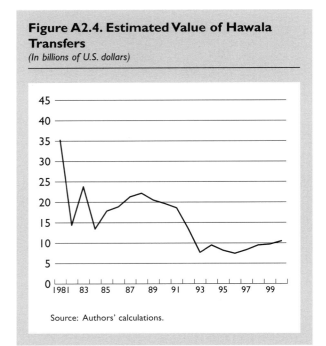

Source: Authors' calculations.

rate policies and more free floating currencies. Between 1989 and 1995, for example, at least 53 countries moved toward more flexible (adjusted according to set of indicators, or managed or independent float) exchange rate regimes.[47]

The model in the paper is a simulation, not an "estimation," model. It merely identifies the black market premium on exchange rates as a key factor in the economic incentives for remitters to use the hawala channel rather than some sanctioned, official channel, for purposes of sending funds to the home country. There are other factors too, such as cultural norms and costs of the official channel, but they can-

not be easily quantified in a time-series sense for purposes of an exercise such as this. Thus, black market premiums show up in the model as the principal variable factor that influences informal remittances, but the intercept and peak used for each country endeavor to capture some other influences.

As for black market premiums, these have been (more or less) measured over the years, and they are given in Table A2.4 for all 15 countries. (Incidentally, roughly the same data have been used recently by Reinhart and Rogoff in their paper on the history of exchange-rate regimes.)[48] The empirical experience shows that, for a number of these countries, this black market premium has tended to decline during the 1990s, but this conclusion does not hold for all of them. It would generally be argued that convergence or unification of formal and informal rates in any country's exchange market represents some improvement in the management of these markets. Usually, this would be the result of policy changes that remove incentives for parallel markets or outright liberalization of official rates and motion toward a floating regime. Thus, it is the empirical evidence on exchange rates (in the sample countries) that suggests there has been some "improvement" in the regimes, but this was not a premise of this experiment.

Given the form of the simulation model, the reduction in overall black market exchange premiums during the 1990s naturally leads to a decline in the relative amount of hawala (compared to total remittances) that the model generates. It was built that way. If other priors are applied to the modeling effort, different results can be generated. Our results are plausible in the coarse sense of showing that the informal channel is potentially "large" when driven by large exchange market incentives, and it tends to recede when costs and incentives in official channels become more favorable. The model results illustrate this.

---

[47]Latter (1996, p. 13).

[48]Reinhart and Rogoff (2002).

Appendix III Regulatory Frameworks for Money Exchange and Remittance Business

Table A3.1. Pakistan

	Money Exchange Business	Money Remittance Business
Regulatory authority	The State Bank is responsible for day-to-day administration of foreign exchange policy, which is exercised through its Exchange Policy Department.	The State Bank is responsible for day-to-day administration of foreign exchange policy, which is exercised through its Exchange Policy Department.
Legal status	Legal: *Foreign Exchange Regulations Act, 1947 and Notifications Issued Hereunder.*	Illegal: *Foreign Exchange Regulations Act, 1947 and Notifications Issued Hereunder.* No person in, or resident in, Pakistan shall make any payment to or for the credit of any person resident outside Pakistan [clause 5 (a)]; draw, issue, or negotiate any bill of exchange or promissory note or acknowledge any debt, so that a right (whether actual or contingent) to receive a payment is created or transferred in favor of any person resident outside Pakistan [5(b)]; make any payment to or for the credit of any person by order or on behalf of any person resident outside Pakistan [5 (c)]; place any sum to the credit of any person resident outside Pakistan [5(d)]; make any payment to or for the credit of any person as consideration for or in association with (1) the receipt by any person of a payment or the acquisition by any person of property outside Pakistan and (2) the creation or transfer in favor of any person of a right whether actual or contingent to receive a payment or acquire property outside Pakistan [5(e)]; draw, issue, or negotiate any bill of exchange or promissory note, transfer any security or acknowledge any debt, so that a right (whether actual or contingent) to receive a payment is created or transferred in favor of any person as consideration for or in association with any matter referred to in clause 5(e) [5(f)].
Licensing/registration: Documentation	1. *Business Plan*: Stating the nature of transactions that are desired to be dealt with. 2. *Management*: Confirmation that trained staff and the required systems and equipment to handle foreign currency transactions are available.	
Permitted activities	1. *Permitted Activities*: No person other than an authorized dealer shall in Pakistan, and no person resident in Pakistan other than an authorized dealer shall outside Pakistan, *buy or borrow from, or sell or lend to, or exchange with*, any person not being an authorized dealer, any foreign exchange. 2. An authorized dealer may have dealings in all foreign currencies or may be restricted to authorizing dealings in specified foreign currencies only; may be authorized to engage in transactions of all	

41

Table A3.1 *(continued)*

	Money Exchange Business	Money Remittance Business
	descriptions in foreign currencies or may be restricted to authorizing specified transactions only; may be granted authority for a specified period, or within specified amounts. 3. No person whether an authorized dealer or otherwise, shall enter into any transaction which provides for the conversion of Pakistan currency into foreign currency or foreign currency into Pakistan currency at rates of exchange *other than the rates for the time being authorized by the State Bank* [clause 4(2)].	
Prudential regulation	1. *Customer Identification Records*: Authorized Operators should, before approving any transactions, satisfy themselves about the bonafides of the applicant and the genuineness of the transaction by verifying the necessary documents. They should ensure that the applications are on the prescribed forms, wherever such forms are prescribed, and are supported by appropriate documentary evidence. In all these cases it will be deemed that they have satisfied themselves about the bonafides of the applicants and the correctness of the statements made by them on the application and the accompanying documents, if any. 2. *Disclosure*: Authorized Operators are required to bring the Foreign Exchange regulations to the notice of their customers and to ensure compliance in their day-to-day operations. 3. *Suspicious Transactions Reports*: Authorized Operators should also report to the State Bank every case of evasion or attempt, direct or indirect, at evasion of the provisions of the Act and Notifications or any rules, orders or directions issued thereunder, immediately as it comes to their notice [3 (4)]. 4. *Prudential Reports*: Authorized Operators must submit to the State Bank returns of their dealings in foreign exchange on due dates in the forms prescribed in the Manual.	
Supervision		1. Where any person is tried for contravening any provision of this Act or of any rule, direction, or order made hereunder which prohibits him from doing an act without permission, the burden of proving that he had the requisite permission shall be on him [24(1)]. 2. If in a case in which the proof of complicity of a person resident in Pakistan with a person outside Pakistan is essential to prove an offense under this Act, then after proof of the circumstances otherwise sufficient to establish the commission of the offense, it shall be presumed that there was such complicity, and the burden of proving that there was no such complicity shall be on the person accused of the offense [24(2)]. 3. Where the person accused of having made any payment in contravention of clause (c) of sub-section (1) of Section 5 is proved to have received from any person outside Pakistan a message which raises a reasonable suspicion that it relates to certain payment to be made, the Tribunal may in the absence of proof to the contrary by the accused person presume that he had made such payment in pursuance of such message [24(3)].

Table A3.1 *(concluded)*

	Money Exchange Business	Money Remittance Business
		4. If, after the issue of a notification under clause (a) of section 9, any person is found to be in possession of, or to have under his control, any foreign exchange specified in the notification, in circumstances which tend to raise a reasonable suspicion that he has contravened the notification, he shall be presumed to have contravened the notification unless he can, by proving the time when and the manner in which the foreign exchange came into his possession or under his control, show that he had not in fact contravened the notification [24(4)].
Revocation, restriction, or variation of license	1. An authorized money changer shall comply with such general or special directions or instructions as the State Bank may, from time to time, think fit to give including those for supply of data, the rate and code of conduct in doing business. Failure to comply with the instructions may lead to suspension of the license or other actions as necessary [3A(4), 3B].	

Source: State Bank of Pakistan, *Foreign Exchange Regulations Act, 1947 and Notifications Issued Hereunder.*

Table A3.2. United Arab Emirates

	Money Exchange Business	Money Remittance Business
Regulatory authority: Legislation	The Central Bank of the U.A.E. 1. Federal Law No. 10 (1980) concerning the Central Bank, monetary system, and organization of banking. 2. Resolution No. 31/2/1986 regarding the regulation of money changing business in the U.A.E. 3. Resolution No. 123/7/92 regarding the regulation of the money changing business in the U.A.E.	The Central Bank of the U.A.E. 1. Federal Law No. 10 (1980) concerning the Central Bank, monetary system, and organization of banking. 2. Resolution No. 31/2/1986 regarding the regulation of money changing business in the U.A.E. 3. Resolution No. 123/7/92 regarding the regulation of the money changing business in the U.A.E.
Licensing/registration: Documentation	1. *Business Plan*: Nature and scale of money changing business, future development plans, including management plans [clause 3(a)]. 2. *Applicant*: Name, address, brief statement about the applicant, copy of passport or of U.A.E. identity card [3(b)]. 3. *Guarantee*: An undertaking to provide a bank guarantee drawn in favor of the Central Bank equal to 50 percent of the capital of the applicant [3(c)]. 4. *Supervision*: An undertaking to comply with all Central Bank resolutions, instructions, directives, and subject the business records to the examination, audit, and supervision of the Central Bank [3(d)]. 5. *Other Documents*: Any other information required by the Central Bank for purposes of processing the application [3(e)].	1. *Business Plan*: Nature and scale of money changing business, future development plans, including management plans [clause 3(a)]. 2. *Applicant*: Name, address, brief statement about the applicant, copy of passport or of U.A.E. identity card [3(b)]. 3. *Guarantee*: An undertaking to provide a bank guarantee drawn in favor of the Central Bank equal to 50 percent of the capital of the applicant [3(c)]. 4. *Supervision*: An undertaking to comply with all Central Bank resolutions, instructions, directives, and subject the business records to the examination, audit, and supervision of the Central Bank [3(d)]. 5. *Other Documents*: Any other information required by the Central Bank for purposes of processing the application [3(e)].
Licensing/registration: Ownership	1. *Paid up Capital*: Dh. 2 million [Article 4(a)] Individuals: The applicant is a U.A.E. national above the age of 21 years [4.2(b)]. 2. *Ownership Structure*: The share of U.A.E. nationals in the company is not less than 60 percent of the total paid up capital [4.2(b)]. No commercial bank is allowed to manage the licensed person whether local or foreign [4.4(c)].	1. *Paid up Capital*: Dh. 2 million [Article 4(a)] Individuals: The applicant is a U.A.E. national above the age of 21 years [4.2(b)]. 2. *Ownership Structure*: The share of U.A.E. nationals in the company is not less than 60 percent of the total paid up capital [4.2(b)]. No commercial bank is allowed to manage the licensed person whether local or foreign [4.4(c)].
Licensing/registration: Fitness and probity test	1. *Personal Reliability*: Be of good conduct and behavior; not convicted of any offense involving dishonor or dishonesty or violence, or have failed to honor his liabilities toward banks or other creditors; shall not have been declared bankrupt or reached a settlement; have had their assets put under judicial receivership [4.3(a)]. 2. *Professional Qualifications*: Must have the appropriate theoretical knowledge of money changing business and the necessary management experience [4.3(b)].	1. *Personal Reliability*: Be of good conduct and behavior; not convicted of any offense involving dishonor or dishonesty or violence, or have failed to honor his liabilities toward banks or other creditors; shall not have been declared bankrupt or reached a settlement; have had their assets put under judicial receivership [4.3(a)]. 2. *Professional Qualifications*: Must have the appropriate theoretical knowledge of money changing business and the necessary management experience [4.3(b)].
Permitted activities	"Money Changing business" means *the purchase and sale of foreign currencies in the form of bank notes and coins, the purchase and sale of travelers checks*, the handling of remittance business in both the local and foreign currencies and other matters approved by the Central Bank.	"Money Changing business" means the purchase and sale of foreign currencies in the form of bank notes and coins, the purchase and sale of travelers checks, *the handling of remittance business in both the local and foreign currencies* and other matters approved by the Central Bank.
Prudential regulation	1. *Capital*: Total assets must not exceed ten times the paid up capital and must not fall below the approved limit [8.1(a)]. Any partner in the business may not withdraw any amount from the business in excess of his share of net annual profits [8.2(l)].	

Table A3.2 *(continued)*

Money Exchange Business	Money Remittance Business
2. *Management*: Managers must always receive prior approval from the Central Bank [8.2(b)]. 3. *Ownership*: The bank's ownership and capital structure should not be altered without Central Bank permission [8.2(c)]. 4. *Organizational Restructuring*: No mergers, amalgamations, or joint ventures without Central Bank permission [8.2(d)]. 5. *Location and Branches*: The premises and change of premises for conducting the business requires central bank approval. *No other activity of whatsoever nature can be undertaken in the same premises* [8.2(e)]. No branches can be opened without Central Bank permission [8.2(g)]. 6. *Business Name*: The business name shall not include the words "bank," "financial institution," "investment/commercial/real estate company," or any other than money changing business [8.2(f)]. 7. *Auditors*: The business must appoint a Central Bank approved auditor [8.2(h)]. 8. *Accounting Records*: The business must maintain proper accounting records and submit these forms as required by the Central Bank [8.2(h)]. The business is authorized to issue drafts in its own name and drafts must be signed by the duly authorized signatories [8.2(j)]. The business shall provide, upon request from the Central Bank, all data, information, or statistics, at any time, and for any specified period, and such information shall be identical to the records of the business and it shall be regarded and treated as confidential. 9. *Transaction Receipts*: Dealings between the business and customers must be supported by official receipts [8.2(i)]. 10. *Disclosure*: Customers must be informed by a public notice their right to a receipt and the rates at which the transactions are conducted [8.2(i)]. 11. *Asset Quality*: The business shall not encumber any assets without the prior permission of the Central Bank [8.2(j)]. 12. *Insider Borrowings*: Shareholders, partners, directors, managers, or controllers of the business may not borrow from or lend to the licensed business and they may not have current accounts or any other accounts with the business [8.2(m)]. 13. *Prudential Reports*: The business is required to submit on a quarterly basis to the Central Bank a signed copy of the year end accounts and the auditors report [8.2(n)].	1. *Capital*: Total assets must not exceed ten times the paid up capital and must not fall below the approved limit [8.1(a)]. Any partner in the business may not withdraw any amount from the business in excess of his share of net annual profits [8.2(l)]. 2. *Management*: Managers must always receive prior approval from the Central Bank [8.2(b)]. 3. *Ownership*: The bank's ownership and capital structure should not be altered without Central Bank permission [8.2(c)]. 4. *Organizational Restructuring*: No mergers, amalgamations, or joint ventures without Central Bank permission [8.2(d)]. 5. *Location and Branches*: The premises and change of premises for conducting the business requires central bank approval. *No other activity of whatsoever nature can be undertaken in the same premises* [8.2(e)]. No branches can be opened without Central Bank permission [8.2(g)]. 6. *Business Name*: The business name shall not include the words "bank," "financial institution," "investment/commercial/real estate company," or any other than money changing business [8.2(f)]. 7. *Auditors*: The business must appoint a Central Bank approved auditor [8.2(h)]. 8. *Accounting Records*: The business must maintain proper accounting records and submit these forms as required by the Central Bank [8.2(h)]. The business is authorized to issue drafts in its own name and drafts must be signed by the duly authorized signatories [8.2(j)]. The business shall provide, upon request from the Central Bank, all data, information, or statistics, at any time, and for any specified period, and such information shall be identical to the records of the business and it shall be regarded and treated as confidential. 9. *Customer Identification Records*: Money changers that are involved in money funds transfers must record details of persons or institutions that transfer an amount of Dh. 2000 (two thousand) or equivalent in other currencies. To ensure the correct identity of the client, any of the following original documents are required: (1) passport, or (2) U.A.E. ID card for U.A.E. nationals, or (3) labor card for non-U.A.E. nationals, or (4) driver's license. With the necessity to carefully check the person's photo in all cases: (1) recording the phone number only (without the address). In the case of transfers in amounts less than Dh. 2000, the transferor should be given a receipt without the said details. 10. *Transaction receipts*: Dealings between the business and customers must be supported by official receipts [8.2(i)]. 11. *Disclosure*: Customers must be informed by a public notice their right to a receipt and the rates at which the transactions are conducted [8.2(i)]. 12. *Asset Quality*: The business shall not encumber any assets without the prior permission of the Central Bank [8.2(j)].

Table A3.2 *(concluded)*

	Money Exchange Business	Money Remittance Business
		13. *Insider Borrowings*: Shareholders, partners, directors, managers, or controllers of the business may not borrow from or lend to the licensed business and they may not have current accounts or any other accounts with the business [8.2(m)]. 14. *Prudential Reports*: The business is required to submit on a quarterly basis to the Central Bank a signed copy of the year end accounts and the auditors report [8.2(n)].
Supervision	The Central Bank reserves the right to inspect the activities of the licensed person at any time it finds it appropriate to ensure adherence to the provisions of its resolutions [9].	The Central Bank reserves the right to inspect the activities of the licensed person at any time it finds it appropriate to ensure adherence to the provisions of its resolutions [9].
Revocation, restriction, or variation of license	The Central Bank may revoke a license if (1) it appears there is a breach of the conditions of the license; (2) the business is in breach of any instructions or circulars issued by the Central Bank; (3) the Central Bank is issued with false, misleading, or inaccurate information from the business; (4) the interests of customers or potential customers of the business are in any other way threatened; (5) a competent judicial authority orders its liquidation; (6) a judicial receiver or manager has been appointed; (7) a bankruptcy order has been made against the business; (8) the business is unable to pay its debts as they fall due; (9) the value of the assets are less than the amount of its liabilities, taking into account its contingent or prospective liabilities.	The Central Bank may revoke a license if (1) it appears there is a breach of the conditions of the license; (2) the business is in breach of any instructions or circulars issued by the Central Bank; (3) the Central Bank is issued with false, misleading, or inaccurate information from the business; (4) the interests of customers or potential customers of the business are in any other way threatened; (5) a competent judicial authority orders its liquidation; (6) a judicial receiver or manager has been appointed; (7) a bankruptcy order has been made against the business; (8) the business is unable to pay its debts as they fall due; (9) the value of the assets are less than the amount of its liabilities, taking into account its contingent or prospective liabilities.

Sources: Central Bank of the United Arab Emirates, Resolution No. 123/7/92 *Regarding the Regulation of Money Changing Business in the U.A.E* and Notice 1815/2001 to *All Money Changers Operating in the U.A.E. on Outgoing Transfers*, dated 01/10/2001.

Appendix IV Examples

Box A4.1. U.A.E. Money Transfer Form for Money Changers

Transferred Amount:

(For outgoing transfers of Dh. 2000 or the equivalent in other currencies or more.)

Method of Payment for Transfer:
Cash
Travelers' Checks

Full Name of Transferor:

ID No.:
Type of ID:
Passport/Nationality:
U.A.E. ID Card/Labor Card:
Driving License (U.A.E.):
Telephone Number:
Name of Beneficiary:
Address of Beneficiary:
Signature of Transferor:

For Use of the Money Changer:

Authorized Signature:
_____

Source: Notice 1815/2001 to *All Money Changers Operating in the U.A.E. on Outgoing Transfers,* dated 01/10/2001.

Box A4.2. Registration Requirements for Money Service Operators in the United Kingdom

(1) A person who, on or after June 1, 2002, acts as a money service operator must be registered by the Commissioners.

(2) Paragraph (1) does not apply to a person who, immediately before June 1, 2002, is acting as a money service operator, provided he has before that date made an application to be registered which has not been determined.

(3) A person to whom this regulation applies must:

(a) make an application to be registered in such manner as the Commissioners may direct; and

(b) furnish the following information to the Commissioners, that is to say:

(i) the applicant's name and (if different) the name of the business;

(ii) the applicant's VAT registration number or, if he is not registered for VAT, any other reference number issued to him by the Commissioners;

(iii) the nature of the business;

(iv) the address of each of the premises at which the applicant carries on (or proposes to carry on) business;

(v) any agency or franchise agreement relating to the business, and the names and addresses of all relevant principals, agents, franchisers, or franchisees;

(vi) the name of the relevant money laundering reporting officer (if any); and

(vii) whether any person concerned (or proposed to be concerned) in the management, control, or operation of the business has been convicted of a money-laundering offense or of money laundering within the meaning of regulation 2(3) of the 1993 Regulations.

(4) At any time after receiving an application to be registered and before determining it, the Commissioners may require the applicant to furnish them, within 21 days beginning with the date of being requested to do so, with such further information as they reasonably consider necessary to enable them to determine the application.

(5) Any information to be furnished to the Commissioners under this regulation must be in such form or verified in such manner as they may specify.

(6) In this regulation, "the business" means money service business which the applicant carries on or proposes to carry on.

Source: The Money Laundering Regulations, 2001, available via the Internet: http://www.hmce.gov.uk/business/othertaxes/stat-instrumsb.pdf.

Bibliography

شيخ عبدالله العلايلي، أين الخطأ؟ تصحيح مفاهيم ونظرة تجديد ، دار الجديد
١٩٩٢ ، بيروت، لبنان، الطبعة الثانية. الطبعة الأولى نشر في دار العلم
للملايين، بيروت ١٩٧٨.

[Sheikh Abdullah Al Allaili, 1992, *Ain Alkhataa, Tas'hih Mafaheem Wa Nazret Tajdeed, Dar Aljadid,* 2nd ed., Beirut; 1978, *Dar, Al Elem Lel Mala Yeen,* 1st ed., Beirut.]

Aggarwal, Chiranjiva Lal, 1966, *The Law of Hundis and Negotiable Instruments,* 8th ed. (Lucknow, India: Eastern Book Company).

Aglietta, Michel, and André Orléan, 2002, *La Monnaie entre Violence et Confiance* (Paris: Odile Jacob).

Al-Suhaimi, Jammaz, 2002, "Demystifying Hawala Business," *Banker* (April), pp. 76–77.

Asia Pacific Group (APG) on Money Laundering Secretariat, 1998, "Money Laundering: The International and Regional Response," Sydney, May.

APG Typologies Working Group on Alternative Remittance & Underground Banking Systems, 2001, "Report for the APG Money Laundering Methods and Typologies Workshop," Singapore, October 17–18.

Carroll, Lisa C., 2001, "Alternative Remittance Systems Distinguishing Sub-systems of Ethnic Money Laundering in Interpol Member Countries on the Asian Continent." Available via the Internet: http://www.interpol.int/Public/FinancialCrime/MoneyLaundering/EthnicMoney.

Caskey, John P., 1994, *Fringe Banking: Check-Cashing Outlets, Pawnshops, and the Poor* (New York: Russell Sage).

Center for Central Banking Studies (CCBS), 1999, "Risk, Cost, and Liquidity in Alternative Payment Systems," *Bank of England Quarterly Bulletin,* February.

Cottle, Michele, 2001, "Hawala vs. the War on Terrorism," *New Republic,* October 15. Available via the Internet: http://www.tnr.com.

Cox, James, 2001, "Hundi System May Foil Investigators," *USA Today,* October 7.

Currency Data and Intelligence, Ltd., various years, *World Currency Yearbook* (formerly *Pick's Currency Yearbook*) (New York: Pick Publishing Corporation).

Department of Foreign Affairs and Trade (Australia), East Asia Analytic Unit, 1994, *India's Economy at the Midnight Hour: Australia's India Strategy* (Canberra: Australian Government Publishing Service).

Dev Raj, Ranjit, 2000, "Budget Fails to Tackle Huge Black Economy," *Asia Times,* March 7.

Economist, 2001, "Cheap and Trusted," November 24, p. 71.

Elbadawi, Ibrahim, and Robert de Rezende Rocha, 1992, "Determinants of Expatriate Workers' Remittances in North Africa and Europe," Policy Research Working Paper No. 1038 (Washington: World Bank).

Financial Action Task Force (FATF) on Money Laundering, various years, "Report on Money Laundering Typologies" (Appendixes to FATF *Annual Reports*) (Paris: FATF Secretariat, Organization for Economic Cooperation and Development). Available via the Internet: http://www1.oecd.org/fatf/FATDocs_en.htm#Annual.

Findeisen, Michael, 2000, *Underground Banking in Germany: Interface Between Illegal "Remittance Services" Within the Meaning of Section 1(1a)(6) of the Banking Act (KWG) and Legal Banking Business,* official document.

Forex Association of Pakistan, 2002, Press Release, January 6.

Fry, Maxwell J., 1974, *The Afghan Economy: Money, Finance, and Critical Constraints to Economic Development* (Leiden, Netherlands: Brill).

G–10 Committee on Banking Regulations & Supervisory Practices, 1988, "Prevention of Criminal Use of the Banking System for the Purpose of Money Laundering," Basel Statement of Principles. Available via Internet: http://www.imolin.org/conventi.htm.

Ganguly, Meenakshi, 2001, "A Banking System Built for Terrorism," *Time,* October 21. Available via the Internet: http://www.time.com/time/magazine/contents.

Grabbe, J. Orlin., 2002, "In Praise of Hawala," *Laissez Faire Electronic Times,* May 13. Available via the Internet: http://freedom.orlingrabbe.com/lfetimes/hawala. htm.

Howlett, Christine, 2000, "Investigation and Control of Money Laundering via Alternative Remittance and Underground Banking Systems" (Canberra: Churchill Trust).

International Monetary Fund, various years, *Annual Report on Exchange Arrangements and Exchange Restrictions* (Washington: International Monetary Fund).

———, 1997a, *India: Recent Economic Developments,* IMF Staff Country Report No. 97/73 (Washington: International Monetary Fund).

———, 1997b, *Pakistan: Recent Economic Developments,* IMF Staff Country Report No. 97/120 (Washington: International Monetary Fund).

———, 1999, *Philippines: Selected Issues,* IMF Staff Country Report No. 99/92 (Washington: International Monetary Fund).

———, 2001a, "Financial System Abuse, Financial Crime, and Money Laundering—Background Paper," IMF Background Paper, February 12.

———, 2001b, *India: Recent Economic Developments and Selected Issues,* IMF Staff Country Report No. 01/81 (Washington: International Monetary Fund).

———, 2001c, *Sri Lanka: Recent Economic Developments,* IMF Staff Country Report No. 01/70 (Washington: International Monetary Fund).

Jost, Patrick, and Harjit Singh Sandhu, 2000, "The Hawala Alternative Remittance System and Its Role in Money Laundering" (Lyon: Interpol General Secretariat). Available via the Internet: http://www.interpol.int/Public/FinancialCrime/MoneyLaundering/hawala.

Kaplan, Edward H., 1997, "Chinese Economic History from Stone Age to Mao's Age" (unpublished; Bellingham: Western Washington University).

Kapoor, Sanjay, 1996, *Bad Money, Bad Politics: The Untold Hawala Story* (New Delhi: Har-Anand).

Kletzer, Kenneth, and Renu Kohli, 2001, "Financial Repression and Exchange Rate Management: Theory and Evidence for India," IMF Working Paper 01/103 (Washington: International Monetary Fund).

Kohli, Renu, 2001, "Capital Flows and Their Macroeconomic Effects in India," IMF Working Paper 01/192 (Washington: International Monetary Fund).

Lambert, Larry, 1996, "Underground Banking and National Security," *Security and Political Risk Analysis India (SAPRA) Bulletin,* March.

Latter, Tony, 1996, *Choice of Exchange Rate Regime* (London: Bank of England, Center for Central Banking Studies).

Luttikhuizen, Ronald, and Brug Kazemier, 1998, "A Systematic Approach to the Hidden and Informal Activities" (Voorburg: Statistics Netherlands).

Maimbo, Samuel M., 1999, "The Money Exchange Dealers of Kabul: A Study of the Informal Funds Transfer Market in Afghanistan" (unpublished; Washington: World Bank).

Miller, Matt, 1999, "Underground Banking," *Institutional Investor Magazine,* January. Available via the Internet http://www.institutionalinvestor.com/platinum/archives.

Pakistan Ministry of Finance, 2000–01, *Economic Survey.*

Passas, Nikos, 2000, "Informal Value Transfer Systems and Criminal Organizations: A Study into So-Called Underground Banking Networks" (The Hague: Netherlands Ministry of Justice).

Pohit, Sanjib, and Nisha Taneja, 2000, "India's Informal Trade with Bangladesh and Nepal: A Qualitative Assessment," Working Paper 58 (New Delhi: Council for Research on International Economic Relations).

Quirk, Peter, 1996, "Macroeconomic Implications of Money Laundering," IMF Working Paper 96/66 (Washington: International Monetary Fund).

Reddy, Y.V., 1997, "Gold Banking in India," address to the World Gold Council Conference, New Delhi, August 2. Reprinted in *BIS Review,* 1997.

Reinhart, Carmen, and Kenneth Rogoff, 2002, "The Modern History of Exchange Rate Arrangements: A Reinterpretation," NBER Working Paper 8963 (Cambridge, Massachusetts: NBER). Available via the Internet: http://papers.nber.org/papers/w8963.pdf.

Rodriguez, Edgard, and Susan Horton, 1995, "International Return Migration and Remittances in the Philippines," Working Paper UT ECIPA Horton 95–01 (Toronto: University of Toronto, Department of Economics).

Saudi Arabian Monetary Agency, 1981, *Rules Regulating the Money Changing Business,* No. 3/920, dated 16–2–1402 (Riyadh), December.

———, 1994, *A Collection of the Monetary and Banking Laws and Regulations* (Riyadh).

Shabsigh, Ghiath, 1995, "The Underground Economy: Estimation and Policy Implications: The Case of Pakistan," IMF Working Paper 95/101 (Washington: International Monetrary Fund).

Sharma, Rajendra, 1997, "Hawala: A Popular Mode of Transactions in Gujarat," *Indian Express.*

Siddiki, Jalal, 2000, "Black Market Exchange Rates in India: An Empirical Analysis," *Empirical Economics,* Vol. 25, pp. 297–313.

State Bank of Pakistan, 2002a, *Annual Report FY 2001.* (Karachi: State Bank of Pakistan).

———, 2002b, *First Quarterly Report for FY 2002* (Karachi: State Bank of Pakistan).

Tanzi, Vito, 1996, "Money Laundering and the International Financial System," IMF Working Paper 96/55 (Washington: International Monetary Fund).

"Underground Forex Market Feels the Pinch," 2001, *Indian Express,* October 5.

United Arab Emirates, 2002, *Abu Dhabi Declaration on Hawala* (Abu Dhabi).

U.S. Customs Service, 1999, *Black Market Peso Exchange: A Trade-Based Money Laundering System* (Washington: U.S. Treasury Department).

U.S. Department of State, Bureau for International Narcotics and Law Enforcement Affairs, 1999, *International Narcotics Control Strategy Report, 1999* (Washington: U.S. Department of State).

U.S. House of Representatives, Committee on Financial Services, 2001, Hearings on Dismantling Terrorist Financial Networks: Testimony of Jimmy Gurule, Treasury Undersecretary for Enforcement, October 3.

U.S. Senate, 2001, "Bayh Amendments Will Starve Terror Groups of Funding in U.S. and Abroad," Press Release, October 4.

U.S. Senate, Committee on Banking, 2001a, Hearings on the Administration's National Money Laundering Strategy: Testimony of Alvin James, September 26.

———, Subcommittee on International Trade and Finance, 2001b, Hearing on Hawala and Underground Financing Terrorist Mechanisms: Testimony of Rahim Bariek, Bariek Money Transfer, November 14.

———, Subcommittee on International Trade and Finance, 2001c, Hearing on Hawala and Underground Terrorist Financing Mechanisms: Prepared Statement of Mr. Patrick Jost, SRA International, November 14.

U.S. Treasury, Financial Crimes Enforcement Network, 1997, "The Colombian Black Market Peso Exchange," Advisory No. 9, November.

Wall Street Journal, 2002, "Money Network Tied to Terrorism Survives Assault," April 22, p. A1.

Wilson, John F., 1992, "Physical Currency Movements and Capital Flows," *Report on the Measurement of International Capital Flows: Background Papers* (Washington: International Monetary Fund), pp. 91–97.

Wood, Adrian, 1988, "Global Trends in Real Exchange Rates: 1960–1984," Discussion Paper No. 35 (Washington: World Bank).

Recent Occasional Papers of the International Monetary Fund

222. Informal Funds Transfer Systems: An Analysis of the Informal Hawala System, by Mohammed El Qorchi, Samuel Munzele Maimbo, and John F. Wilson. 2003.

221. Deflation: Determinants, Risks, and Policy Options, by Manmohan S. Kumar, Taimur Baig, Jörg Decressin, Chris Faulkner-MacDonagh, and Tarhan Feyzioğlu. 2003.

220. Effects of Financial Globalization on Developing Countries: Some Empirical Evidence, by Eswar S. Prasad, Kenneth Rogoff, Shang-Jin Wei, and Ayhan Kose. 2003.

219. Economic Policy in a Highly Dollarized Economy: The Case of Cambodia, by Mario de Zamaroczy and Sopanha Sa. 2003.

218. Fiscal Vulnerability and Financial Crises in Emerging Market Economies, by Richard Hemming, Michael Kell, and Axel Schimmelpfennig. 2003.

217. Managing Financial Crises: Recent Experience and Lessons for Latin America, edited by Charles Collyns and G. Russell Kincaid. 2003.

216. Is the PRGF Living Up to Expectations?—An Assessment of Program Design, by Sanjeev Gupta, Mark Plant, Benedict Clements, Thomas Dorsey, Emanuele Baldacci, Gabriela Inchauste, Shamsuddin Tareq, and Nita Thacker. 2002.

215. Improving Large Taxpayers' Compliance: A Review of Country Experience, by Katherine Baer. 2002.

214. Advanced Country Experiences with Capital Account Liberalization, by Age Bakker and Bryan Chapple. 2002.

213. The Baltic Countries: Medium-Term Fiscal Issues Related to EU and NATO Accession, by Johannes Mueller, Christian Beddies, Robert Burgess, Vitali Kramarenko, and Joannes Mongardini. 2002.

212. Financial Soundness Indicators: Analytical Aspects and Country Practices, by V. Sundararajan, Charles Enoch, Armida San José, Paul Hilbers, Russell Krueger, Marina Moretti, and Graham Slack. 2002.

211. Capital Account Liberalization and Financial Sector Stability, by a staff team led by Shogo Ishii and Karl Habermeier. 2002.

210. IMF-Supported Programs in Capital Account Crises, by Atish Ghosh, Timothy Lane, Marianne Schulze-Ghattas, Aleš Bulíř, Javier Hamann, and Alex Mourmouras. 2002.

209. Methodology for Current Account and Exchange Rate Assessments, by Peter Isard, Hamid Faruqee, G. Russell Kincaid, and Martin Fetherston. 2001.

208. Yemen in the 1990s: From Unification to Economic Reform, by Klaus Enders, Sherwyn Williams, Nada Choueiri, Yuri Sobolev, and Jan Walliser. 2001.

207. Malaysia: From Crisis to Recovery, by Kanitta Meesook, Il Houng Lee, Olin Liu, Yougesh Khatri, Natalia Tamirisa, Michael Moore, and Mark H. Krysl. 2001.

206. The Dominican Republic: Stabilization, Structural Reform, and Economic Growth, by Alessandro Giustiniani, Werner C. Keller, and Randa E. Sab. 2001.

205. Stabilization and Savings Funds for Nonrenewable Resources, by Jeffrey Davis, Rolando Ossowski, James Daniel, and Steven Barnett. 2001.

204. Monetary Union in West Africa (ECOWAS): Is It Desirable and How Could It Be Achieved? by Paul Masson and Catherine Pattillo. 2001.

203. Modern Banking and OTC Derivatives Markets: The Transformation of Global Finance and Its Implications for Systemic Risk, by Garry J. Schinasi, R. Sean Craig, Burkhard Drees, and Charles Kramer. 2000.

202. Adopting Inflation Targeting: Practical Issues for Emerging Market Countries, by Andrea Schaechter, Mark R. Stone, and Mark Zelmer. 2000.

201. Developments and Challenges in the Caribbean Region, by Samuel Itam, Simon Cueva, Erik Lundback, Janet Stotsky, and Stephen Tokarick. 2000.

200. Pension Reform in the Baltics: Issues and Prospects, by Jerald Schiff, Niko Hobdari, Axel Schimmelpfennig, and Roman Zytek. 2000.

199. Ghana: Economic Development in a Democratic Environment, by Sérgio Pereira Leite, Anthony Pellechio, Luisa Zanforlin, Girma Begashaw, Stefania Fabrizio, and Joachim Harnack. 2000.

198. Setting Up Treasuries in the Baltics, Russia, and Other Countries of the Former Soviet Union: An Assessment of IMF Technical Assistance, by Barry H. Potter and Jack Diamond. 2000.

197. Deposit Insurance: Actual and Good Practices, by Gillian G.H. Garcia. 2000.

196. Trade and Trade Policies in Eastern and Southern Africa, by a staff team led by Arvind Subramanian, with Enrique Gelbard, Richard Harmsen, Katrin Elborgh-Woytek, and Piroska Nagy. 2000.

195. The Eastern Caribbean Currency Union—Institutions, Performance, and Policy Issues, by Frits van Beek, José Roberto Rosales, Mayra Zermeño, Ruby Randall, and Jorge Shepherd. 2000.

194. Fiscal and Macroeconomic Impact of Privatization, by Jeffrey Davis, Rolando Ossowski, Thomas Richardson, and Steven Barnett. 2000.

193. Exchange Rate Regimes in an Increasingly Integrated World Economy, by Michael Mussa, Paul Masson, Alexander Swoboda, Esteban Jadresic, Paolo Mauro, and Andy Berg. 2000.

192. Macroprudential Indicators of Financial System Soundness, by a staff team led by Owen Evans, Alfredo M. Leone, Mahinder Gill, and Paul Hilbers. 2000.

191. Social Issues in IMF-Supported Programs, by Sanjeev Gupta, Louis Dicks-Mireaux, Ritha Khemani, Calvin McDonald, and Marijn Verhoeven. 2000.

190. Capital Controls: Country Experiences with Their Use and Liberalization, by Akira Ariyoshi, Karl Habermeier, Bernard Laurens, Inci Ötker-Robe, Jorge Iván Canales Kriljenko, and Andrei Kirilenko. 2000.

189. Current Account and External Sustainability in the Baltics, Russia, and Other Countries of the Former Soviet Union, by Donal McGettigan. 2000.

188. Financial Sector Crisis and Restructuring: Lessons from Asia, by Carl-Johan Lindgren, Tomás J.T. Baliño, Charles Enoch, Anne-Marie Gulde, Marc Quintyn, and Leslie Teo. 1999.

187. Philippines: Toward Sustainable and Rapid Growth, Recent Developments and the Agenda Ahead, by Markus Rodlauer, Prakash Loungani, Vivek Arora, Charalambos Christofides, Enrique G. De la Piedra, Piyabha Kongsamut, Kristina Kostial, Victoria Summers, and Athanasios Vamvakidis. 2000.

186. Anticipating Balance of Payments Crises: The Role of Early Warning Systems, by Andrew Berg, Eduardo Borensztein, Gian Maria Milesi-Ferretti, and Catherine Pattillo. 1999.

185. Oman Beyond the Oil Horizon: Policies Toward Sustainable Growth, edited by Ahsan Mansur and Volker Treichel. 1999.

184. Growth Experience in Transition Countries, 1990–98, by Oleh Havrylyshyn, Thomas Wolf, Julian Berengaut, Marta Castello-Branco, Ron van Rooden, and Valerie Mercer-Blackman. 1999.

183. Economic Reforms in Kazakhstan, Kyrgyz Republic, Tajikistan, Turkmenistan, and Uzbekistan, by Emine Gürgen, Harry Snoek, Jon Craig, Jimmy McHugh, Ivailo Izvorski, and Ron van Rooden. 1999.

182. Tax Reform in the Baltics, Russia, and Other Countries of the Former Soviet Union, by a staff team led by Liam Ebrill and Oleh Havrylyshyn. 1999.

181. The Netherlands: Transforming a Market Economy, by C. Maxwell Watson, Bas B. Bakker, Jan Kees Martijn, and Ioannis Halikias. 1999.

180. Revenue Implications of Trade Liberalization, by Liam Ebrill, Janet Stotsky, and Reint Gropp. 1999.

179. Disinflation in Transition: 1993–97, by Carlo Cottarelli and Peter Doyle. 1999.

178. IMF-Supported Programs in Indonesia, Korea, and Thailand: A Preliminary Assessment, by Timothy Lane, Atish Ghosh, Javier Hamann, Steven Phillips, Marianne Schulze-Ghattas, and Tsidi Tsikata. 1999.

177. Perspectives on Regional Unemployment in Europe, by Paolo Mauro, Eswar Prasad, and Antonio Spilimbergo. 1999.

176. Back to the Future: Postwar Reconstruction and Stabilization in Lebanon, edited by Sena Eken and Thomas Helbling. 1999.

175. Macroeconomic Developments in the Baltics, Russia, and Other Countries of the Former Soviet Union, 1992–97, by Luis M. Valdivieso. 1998.

174. Impact of EMU on Selected Non-European Union Countries, by R. Feldman, K. Nashashibi, R. Nord, P. Allum, D. Desruelle, K. Enders, R. Kahn, and H. Temprano-Arroyo. 1998.

Note: For information on the titles and availability of Occasional Papers not listed, please consult the IMF's *Publications Catalog* or contact IMF Publication Services.